BALANCE
Living With Life's Demands

Tracey L. Henderson

Abingdon Press
Nashville

Balance: Living With Life's Demands
20/30: Bible Study for Young Adults

by Tracey L. Henderson

Copyright © 2001 by Abingdon Press

ISBN 13: 978-0-687-09761-6

This book is printed on acid-free paper.

MANUFACTURED IN THE UNITED STATES OF AMERICA.

07 08 09 10—10 9 8

CONTENTS

MEET THE WRITER

Tracey L. Henderson is a candidate for ministry as an ordained deacon in The United Methodist Church and has studied at Garrett-Evangelical Theological Seminary in Illinois. In addition to her theological studies, Tracey has an extensive background in agronomics and holds a Ph.D. in agriculture and related sciences. She has served in ministry in the Peace Corps, the Congo, Mozambique, and the United States.

Tracey is active in the local church as well and has served by coordinating small group ministries, developing small groups, leading studies, and writing curriculum. Her seminary emphasis is in Christian education, specializing in mission education and adult ministries.

WELCOME TO 20/30: BIBLE STUDY FOR YOUNG ADULTS

The *20/30* Bible study series is offered for post-modern adults who want to participate in and help structure their own discoveries—in life, in relationships, in faith. In each of the volumes of this series, we will have the opportunity to use our own experience in life and faith to examine the biblical texts in new ways. We will examine biblical images that shape all of our lives, even if we are not immediately aware that they do.

Image Is Everything

Images are what shape our decisions. We may think or know certain important data that weigh heavily in a decision. We may value the advice and counsel of others. We may find that the stated or implied wishes of others influence what we do. But in the end, it is often the *image* we hold that makes the decision.

For example, perhaps you were deeply hurt by someone important to you—an employer, a friend, even a pastor. You know in your heart that the institution is not to blame or that friendships are based on more than one event. But the image shaped by the difficult experience is that the job, or the friend, or the church cannot be relied upon. You *know* better, but you just have to make a change anyway. The image was more powerful than the reason.

Images are powerful, and they are familiar. In each of the studies in this series, you will encounter a well-known image that will connect your familiar experiences with some basis in Scripture.

You juggle multiple demands—school or work, family, friends, church, day-to-day "stuff" like paying bills and dealing with junk mail—but do these activities each receive the proper priority at the proper time? *Balance: Living With Life's Demands* will help you sort through various claims on your life and put your priorities into a healthy and manageable perspective.

You define for yourself what you think is "the good life." Is your definition complete? *Abundance: Living Responsibly With God's Gifts* will guide you into the biblical understanding of abundant life and help you sort out many of the faithful and practical issues that come together in a life of abundance.

You love and are loved in return, and you know this is more than just a matter of emotion. *Love: Opening Your Heart to God and Others* will guide you into the biblical understanding of love and help you explore many facets of love, and love gone wrong, with God, family, friends, and life partner.

You have faith, but you may also realize that it can mean many things. Is it belief or trust, or waiting, or moral behavior, or something else? Or is it all those things? *Faith: Living a Spirited Life* helps you examine your faith and grow as a Christian.

You know what it is like to make agreements, to establish commitments, to give your word and expect to be trusted. *Covenant: Making Commitments That Count* engages you in study sessions that explain a variety of covenants, what happens when covenants are broken, how to have a faithful covenant to care for others and for the earth; and certainly, what it means to have this sacred covenant with God.

You know what it is like to move to a new place, to have to deal with transitions in school or work or in relationships. You have probably experienced changes in your family as you have grown up and moved out on your own. Some of these moves are gradual, just taken in stride. Others can be painful or abrupt; certainly life-changing. In *Exodus: Leaving Behind, Moving On*, you will appreciate learning how God is in the midst of those movements, no matter how minor or how transformational.

You know how important it is to have a sense of support and roots; to have friends and a life partner. *Community: Living Faithfully With Others* introduces you to Scriptures and life examples that delve into intimacy, work and family relationships, and more.

Experience, Faith, Growth, and Action

Each volume in this series will help you probe, on your own terms, how your experience links with your faith and how deepening your faith develops your life experience. If you need a prompt for your reflection, each volume has several pages of real-life case studies. As your faith and commitment to Jesus Christ grow, you may be looking for ways to be involved in specific service opportunities. Several are listed on pages 79-80.

We hope this series will help you encounter God through Scripture, reflection, and dialogue with others who desire to grow in faith, and to serve others. One image we hold is that God is in all things. God is certainly with you.

HOW TO USE THIS RESOURCE

Each session of this resource includes similar components or elements:

- A statement of the issue or question to be explored
- Several "voices" of persons who are currently dealing with that issue
- Exploration of biblical passages relative to the question raised
- "Biblical Studies 101" boxes that provide insight about the study of the Bible
- Questions for reflection and discussion
- Suggested individual and group activities designed to bring the session to life
- Optional case studies (found in the back of the book)
- Various service learning activities related to the session (found in the back of the book)

Choices, Choices, Choices

Collectively, these components mean one thing: *choice*. You have choices to make concerning how to use each session of this resource. Want just the nitty-gritty Bible reading, reflection, and study for personal or group use? Then focus your attention on just those components during your study time.

Like starting with real-life stories about issues then moving into how the Bible might be relevant? Start with the "voices" and move on from there. Use the "voices" to encourage group members to speak about their own experiences.

Prefer highly charged discussion encounters where many different viewpoints can be heard? Start the session with the biblical passages, followed by the questions and group activities. Be sure to compare the ideas found in the "Biblical Studies 101" boxes with your current ideas for more discussion. Want the major challenge of applying biblical principles to a difficult problem? After reading the biblical material, read one of the case studies, using the guidelines provided on page 14, or get involved with one of the service learning options described on pages 79-80.

Great Versatility

This resource has been designed for many different uses. Some persons will use this resource for personal study and reflection. Others will want to explore the work with a small group of friends. And still other folk will see this book as a different type of Sunday school resource.

Spend some time thinking about your own questions, study habits, and learning styles or those of your small group. Then use the guidelines mentioned above to fashion each session into a unique Bible study session to meet those requirements.

Highly Participatory

As you will see, the Scriptures, "voices," commentary, and experience of group members will provide an opportunity for an active, engaging time together. The greatest challenge for a group leader might be "crowd control" —being sure everyone has the chance to put his or her ideas into the mix!

The Scriptures will help you and those who study with you to make connections between real-life issues and the Bible. This resource values and encourages personal participation as a means to understand fully and appreciate the intersection of personal belief with God's ongoing work in each and every life.

ON ORGANIZING A SMALL GROUP

Learning with a small group of persons offers certain advantages over studying by yourself. First, you will hopefully encounter different opinions and ideas, making the experience of Bible study a richer and more challenging event. Second, any leadership responsibilities can be shared among group members. Third, different persons will bring different talents. Some will be deep thinkers while other group members will be creative giants. Some persons will be newcomers to the Bible; their questions and comments will help others clarify their deeply held assumptions.

So how does one go about forming a small group? Follow the steps below and see how easy this task can be.

- **Read through the resource carefully.** Think about the ideas presented, the questions raised, and the exercises suggested. If the sessions of this work excite you, it will be easier for you to spread your enthusiasm to others.

- **Spend some time thinking about church members, friends, and coworkers who might find the sessions of this resource interesting**. On a sheet of paper, list two characteristics or talents you see in each person that would make him or her an attractive Bible study group member. Some talents might include "deep thinker," "creative wizard," or "committed Christian." Remember: The best small group has members who differ in learning styles, talents, ideas, and convictions, but who respect the dignity and integrity of the other members.

- **Most functional small groups have seven to fifteen members.** Make a list of potential group members that doubles your target number. For instance, if you would like a small group of seven to ten members, be prepared to invite fourteen to twenty persons.

- **Once your list of potential candidates is complete, decide on a tentative location and time.** Of course, the details can be negotiated with those persons who accept the invitation, but you need to sound definitive and clear to perspective group members. "We will initially set Wednesday night from 7 to 9 p.m. at my house for our meeting time" will sound more attractive than "Well, I don't know either when or where we would be meeting, but I hope you will consider joining us."

- **Make initial contact with prospective group members short, sweet, and to the point.** Say something like, "We are putting together a Bible study using a different kind of resource. When would be a good time to show you the resource and talk about the study?" Establishing a special time to make the invitation takes the pressure off the prospective group member to make a quick decision.

- **Show up at the decided time and place.** Talk with each prospective member individually. Bring a copy of the resource with you. Show each person what excites you about the study and mention the two unique characteristics or talents you feel he or she would offer the group. Tell each person the initial meeting time and location and how many weeks the small group will meet. Also mention that the need for a new time or location could be discussed during the first group meeting. Ask for a commitment to come to the first session. Thank individuals for their time.

- **Give a quick phone call or e-mail to thank all persons for their consideration and interest.** Remind persons of the time and location of the first meeting.

- **Be organized.** Use the first group meeting to get acquainted. Briefly describe the seven sessions. Have a book for each group member, and discuss sharing responsibilities for leadership.

LEADING AND
SHARING LEADERSHIP

So the responsibility to lead the group has fallen upon you? Don't sweat it. Follow these simple suggestions and you will razzle and dazzle the group with your expertise.

- **Read the session carefully.** Look up all the Bible passages. Take careful notes about the ideas, statements, questions, and activities in the session. Try all the activities.

- **Using twenty to twenty-five blank index cards, write one idea, activity, Bible passage, or question from the session on each card** until you either run out of material or cards. Be sure to look at the case studies and service learning options.

- **Spend a few moments thinking about the members of your group.** How many like to think about ideas, concepts, or problems? How many need to "feel into" an idea by storytelling, worship, prayer, or group activities? Who are the "actors" who prefer a hands-on or participatory approach, such as an art project or simulation, to grasp an idea? List the names of all group members, and record whether you believe each to be a THINKER, FEELER, or ACTOR.

- **Place all the index cards in front of you in the order in which they originally appeared in the session.** Looking at that order, ask yourself: 1) Where is the "Head" of the session—the key ideas or concepts? 2) Where is the "Heart" of the session in which persons will have a deep feeling response? 3) Where are the "feet"—those activities that ask the group to put the ideas and feelings to use? Separate the cards into three stacks: HEAD, HEART, and FEET.

- **Now construct the "body" for your class.** Shift the cards around, using a balance of HEAD, HEART, and FEET cards to determine which activities you will do and in what order. This will be your group's unique lesson plan. Try to choose as many cards as you have group members. Then, match the cards: HEAD and THINKERS; HEART and FEELERS; FEET and ACTORS for each member of the group. Don't forget a card for yourself. If your group has ten members, you should have about ten cards.

- **Develop the leadership plan.** Invite these group members prior to the session to assist in the leadership. Show them the unique lesson plan you developed. Ask for their assistance in developing and/or leading each segment of the session as well as an ice-breaking introduction and a closing ritual or worship experience.

   Your lesson plan should start with welcoming the participants. Hopefully everyone will have read the session ahead of time. Then, begin to move through the activity cards in the order of your unique session plan, sharing the leadership as you have agreed.

   You may have chosen to have all the HEAD activities together, followed by the HEART cards. This would introduce the session's content, followed by helping group members "feel into" the issue through interactive stories, questions, and exercises with all group members. Feel free to add more storytelling, discussion, prayer, meditation, or worship.

   You may next have chosen to use the FEET cards to end the session. Ask the group, "What difference should this session make in our daily lives?" You or the ACTORS should introduce the FEET cards as possible ways to discern a response. Ensuring that group members leave with a few practical suggestions for doing something different during the week is the point of this section of the unique lesson plan.

- **Remember: Leading the group does not mean "Do it all yourself."** With a little planning, you can enlist the talents of many group members. By inviting group members to lead parts of the session that feel comfortable for them, you will model and encourage shared leadership. Welcome their interests in music, prayer, worship, Bible, and so on, to develop innovative and creative Bible study sessions that can transform lives in the name of Jesus Christ.

CHOOSING TEACHING OPTIONS

This young adult series was designed, written, and produced out of an understanding of the attributes, concerns, joys, and faith issues of young adults. With great care and integrity, this image-based print resource was developed to connect biblical events and relationships with contemporary, real-life situations of young adults. Its pages will promote Christian relationships and community, support new biblical learning, encourage spiritual development, and empower faithful decision-making and action.

This study is well-suited to young adults and may be used confidently and effectively. But with the great diversity within the young adult population, not every line of this study will be written "just for you." To be most relevant, some portions of the study material need to be tailored to fit your particular group. Adjustments for a good fit involve making choices from options offered by the resource. This customizing may be done easily by a designated leader who is familiar with the layout of the resource and the young adults who are using it.

What to Expect

In this study Scripture and real-life images mesh together to provoke a personal response. Young adults will find themselves thinking, feeling, imagining, questioning, making decisions, professing faith, building connections, inviting discipleship, taking action, and making a difference. Scripture is at the core of each session. Scenarios weave in the dimensions of real life. Narrative and text boxes frame plenty of teaching options to offer young adults.

Each session is part of a cohesive volume, but it is designed to stand alone. One session is not dependent on knowledge or experience accumulated from other sessions. A group leader can freely choose from the teaching options in an individual session without wondering about how it might affect the other sessions.

A Good Fit

For a better fit, alter the session based on what is known about the young adult participants. Young adults are a diverse constituency with varied experiences, interests, needs, and values. There is really no single defining characteristic that links young adults. Specific information about the age, employment status, household, personal relationships, and lifestyle among participants will equip a leader to make choices that ensure a good fit.

- **Customize.** Read through the session. Notice how scenarios and teaching options move from integrating Scripture and real-life dimensions to inviting a response.

- **Look at the scenario(s).** How real is the presentation of real life? Say that the main character is a professional, white male, married, in his early twenties, and caught in a workplace dilemma that entangles his immediate superior and a subordinate from his division. Perhaps your group members are mostly college students and recent graduates, unmarried, and still on the way to being "settled." There are many differences between the man in the scenario and these group members.

  As a leader, you could choose to eliminate the case study, substitute it with another scenario (there are several more choices on pages 76-78), claim the validity of the dilemma and shift the spotlight from the main character to the subordinate, or modify the description of the main character. Break-out groups based on age or employment experience might also be used to accommodate the differences and offer a better fit.

- **Look at the teaching options.** How are the activities propelling participants toward a personal response? Perhaps the Scripture study requires more meditative quiet than is possible and a more academic, verbal, or artistic approach would offer a better fit. Maybe more direct decisions or actions would fit better than more passive or logical means. Try to keep a balance, though, that allows participants to "get out of their head" to reflect and also to move toward action.

  Conceivably, there could just be too much in any one session. As a leader, you can pick and choose among teaching options, substitute case studies, take two meetings to do one session, and adapt any process to make a better fit. The tailoring process can be evaluated as adjustments are made. Judge the fit every time you meet. Ask questions that gauge relevance, and assess how the resource has stretched minds, encouraged discipleship, and changed lives.

USING BREAK-OUT GROUPS

20/30 break-out groups are small groups that encourage the personal sharing of lives and the gospel. The word *break-out* is a sweeping term that includes a variety of small group settings. A break-out group may resemble a Bible study group, an interest group, a sharing group, or other types of Christian fellowship groups.

Break-out groups offer young adults a chance to belong and personally relate to one another. Members are known, nurtured, and heard by others. Young adults may agree and disagree while maximizing the exchange of ideas, information, or options. They might explore, confront, and resolve personal issues and feelings with empathy and support. Participants can challenge and hold each other accountable to a personalized faith and stretch its links to real life and service.

Forming Break-out Groups

The nature of these small break-out groups will depend on the context and design of the specific session. On occasion the total group of participants will be divided for a particular activity. Break-out groups will differ from one session to the next. Variations may involve the size of the group, how group members are divided, or the task of the group. Break-out groups may also be used to accommodate differences and help tailor the session plan for a better fit. In some sessions, specific group assembly instructions will be provided. For other sessions, decisions regarding the size or division of small groups will be made by the designated leader. Break-out groups may be in the form of pairs or trios, family-sized groups of three to six members, or groups of up to ten members.

They may be arranged simply by grouping persons seated next to one another or in more intentional ways by common interests, characteristics, or life experience. Consider creating break-out groups according to age; gender; type of household, living arrangements, or love relationships; vocation, occupation, career, or employment status; common or built-in connections; lifestyle; values or perspective; or personal interests or traits.

Membership

The membership of break-out groups will vary from session to session, or even within specific sessions. Young adults need to work at knowing and

15

being known, so that there can be a balance between break-out groups that are more similar and those that reflect greater diversity. There may be times when more honest communication, trust, or accountability may be desired and group leaders will need to be free to self-select members for small groups.

It is important for 20/30 break-out groups to practice acceptance and to value the worth of others. The potential for small groups to encourage personal sharing and significant relationships is enhanced when members agree to exercise active listening skills, keep confidences, expect authenticity, foster trust, and develop ways of loving one another. All group members contribute to the development and function of break-out groups. Designated leaders especially need to model manners of hospitality and help ensure that each group member is respected.

Invitational Listening

Consider establishing an "invitational listening" routine that validates the perspective and affirms the voice of each group member. After a question or statement is posed, pause and allow time to think—not all persons think on their feet or talk out loud to think. Then, initiate conversation by inviting one group member, by name, to talk. This person may either choose to talk or to "pass." Either way, this person is honored and is offered an opportunity to speak and be heard. This person carries on the ritual by inviting another group member, by name, to speak. The process continues until all have been invited, by name, to talk. As each one invites another, the responsibility of acceptance and hospitality in the break-out groups is shared among all its members.

Study group members break-out to belong, to share the gospel, to care, and to watch over one another in Christian love. "So deeply do we care for you that we are determined to share with you not only the gospel of God but also our own selves, because you have become very dear to us" (1 Thessalonians 2:8).

BALANCE:
LIVING WITH LIFE'S DEMANDS

What does it mean to live a Christian life? If you asked a hundred Christians this question, you might hear a hundred different answers, but common responses would probably include some of these ideas:

- loving and worshiping God
- being a caring friend
- making an honest living
- living life to the fullest

- being a devoted family member
- reaching out to people in need
- working for justice in the world
- giving sacrificially

When we look at this list, our Christian responsibilities may seem overwhelming. In our fast-paced culture, many of us have our hands full just trying to get by. How can we possibly be good Christians on top of everything else? And how do we do so without neglecting our own needs?

Most of us face a variety of demands on our time, energy, money and/or inner resources. Sometimes the effort to fulfill all of our responsibilities can feel like a losing battle, especially when they appear to compete with each other. We may feel torn between the expectations of our families, friends, employers, and church. We may struggle with how to weigh our obligations to others against our own personal needs and wants. Perhaps we agonize over the plight of the world's poor but feel powerless to change their situation. And in the midst of everything else we have to do, we may wonder how can we ever find time to spend with God.

As we try to keep up with all the things we need and want to accomplish, it is easy to lose touch with what is truly meaningful in our lives. This volume will explore how we, as Christians, can find balance among so many competing demands. We will learn to sort through our various responsibilities and desires, and view them from the perspective of how God calls us to live. Using the Bible as a guide, we will examine Christian teachings about balanced living and apply them to our own situations.

Biblical Perspectives on Balanced Living

The Bible does not use the actual word *balance*, but Scripture certainly has a great deal to teach us on the topic of balanced Christian living. For example, throughout his life Jesus had to balance family obligations, demands of the crowds who followed him, expectations of his disciples and threats from the religious establishment, while always remaining true to God's mission.

This volume will allow us to read and analyze what the Bible has to say about various aspects of balance. Each session will provide opportunities for us to apply biblical teachings to our personal situations. Through activities and discussion questions, we will take a fresh look at some of our own balance issues, explore biblical parallels to them, and discern new insights or answers from Scripture. Each session will end with a challenge to take specific action that will lead us toward a more balanced life.

Balance: From Personal Wholeness to Global Justice

The biblical concept of balance is relevant to us as individuals, people in close personal relationships, members of communities, and citizens of the world. In Session 1, we will discuss what balance means to us and assess the degree of balance in our own lives. Session 2 explores how time pressure detracts from balanced living, and helps us prioritize our time for God, others, and ourselves. Finding balance between our everyday responsibilities and our desire for novelty and adventure is the topic of Session 3. Session 4 shows us how a strong relationship with God can help us to lead a more balanced life. We will examine balance issues in our close personal relationships in Session 5. Session 6 focuses on the biblical concept of justice and our responses to injustice in our everyday experience. The last session will extend the concept of justice to a global scale and explore a biblical vision of balance for all of God's creation.

Journeying Toward Balance

Balance is not something we can accomplish once and be done with. It is not something we can ever cross off on our checklist of things to do. It is not something we will possess at the completion of this study. It will not erase the many responsibilities and stresses in our lives. Instead, balance is a way of living faithfully in the midst of all of life's demands. It is a way of life that is focused on God. Making God our central focus helps us put our other responsibilities in proper perspective. The closer our lives correspond to God's way of living, the more balanced our lives will be.

Unfortunately, we cannot simply snap our fingers and start leading a completely godly life. Striving to find balance will be an ongoing challenge that will undoubtedly involve change. We may need to alter how we view our responsibilities and learn to see competing demands as complementary. We may need courage to leave our comfort zones and consider new possibilities for our lives. We may need to leave behind some unhealthy habits. We may need to transform the ways we are in relationship with others who share in God's creation. We may even find that our whole worldview will change. But the effort will be well worth it.

Consider this study an adventure. May God bless you on the journey.

GOTTA TAKE CARE OF BUSINESS

This session will explore the concept of balance and its importance in the Christian life.

GETTING STARTED

Amanda: Balance is a myth. I grew up with the message that if I worked really hard, I could have it all. But now I do have it all— a great career, a loving husband, two beautiful kids, friends, and money—and my life is so frenzied, it's hard to enjoy it. I'm so exhausted! Why didn't anyone tell me it would be this hard?

Sam: I try to lead a balanced life, but it's hard. I have a lot of homework, two jobs to pay for tuition, plus working out to stay in shape. On weekend nights I go out with my friends—a guy's got to have some fun, right? I guess I should make some time for church, but I can't fit it in. Maybe after graduation.

Jacinta: When I think of balance, I think about relationships. For the past few months with my boyfriend it's been all give and no take. I know Jesus said it's more blessed to give than to receive, but is this what he meant?

Greet one another and introduce yourselves. Then rate how balanced your life is on a scale from 1 to 10, with 10 being a fully balanced life. Share your rating with the rest of the group. Name something about your lifestyle that contributes to balance and something that detracts from it.

Can you identify with the situations of any of the five people in the opening dialogue? In what way(s)? Or do you have an example from your own life to share? What is the major balance issue in each situation? What could each person in the dialogue (or you, if you are sharing your own example) do to achieve a more balanced life?

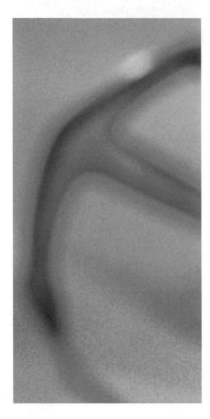

Christa: So far, all we've talked about is balance in our own lives. What about the rest of the world? I have so much and others have so little. Where's the balance in that? I see those pictures of starving kids in Africa, and I feel so guilty. But there's nothing I can do about it—the problems are just too big.

Jake: I don't have the luxury of thinking about balance. The "have-nots" of the world aren't just living on some other continent; we're right here. I work the night shift and have a part-time day job, so I never see my wife and kids. When I'm struggling just to pay the rent every month, how can I think about balance for others? Even balance for myself seems like an impossible dream.

IT'S OUT OF CONTROL!

Our culture worships youth, speed, and money, and the pace of life becomes more and more hectic with every passing year. Many people are run so ragged trying to juggle the expectations of work, school, family, friends, and community that they feel they can no longer cope. For others, the relentless pursuit of pleasure makes even leisure time stressful.

The effects of all these stresses can be tragic. Nearly half of U.S. marriages end in divorce, and suicide is the number three cause of death among young people ages 15-24. A recent survey conducted by psychologists at Indiana University indicated that over a quarter of Americans have felt close to a nervous breakdown related to stress, depression, or anxiety. When we feel like our lives are coming apart at the seams, even if we cannot articulate the cause, we long for some sort of balance.

SMALL GROUP

It's Out of Control
In pairs, share a story about a time in your life when you felt as though your life was out of control. What was out of balance? How did your life situation get out of hand? If the personal situation you describe was in your past, tell if and how you resolved it. If you are currently experiencing the situation, share your vision of the balanced life you would like to have. How did (or does) your faith influence your response to the situation?

BALANCE: WHAT IS IT?

What is a balanced life for a Christian? How can we "take care of business" and still be a complete person? Although the actual word *balance* does not appear in the Bible in the sense in which we are using it here, the concept certainly does.

Read Mark 5:21-43 and Luke 8:26-39. Both passages show Jesus engaged in a traveling preaching ministry around the Sea of Galilee. When Jesus encountered people in great distress, he took the time to heal them and make them whole. These and other healing stories suggest that healing and wholeness in the biblical sense refer not just to physical health, but overall well-being and balance of body, mind, and spirit.

Balance: What Is It?
As a group, make a "balance" word web. Start with a chalkboard, a marker-board, or a large piece of newsprint and write the word *balance* in the center. Then have one person draw a line coming off of the word *balance* and, at the end of the line, write the first word that comes to mind. Each subsequent person should write another word associated either with the original word (*balance*) or any of the other words coming off of it. Take several turns, then discuss the results. What insights did you gain about your concept of the balanced life?
(As a variation, have two groups; one to do a web for *balance*, the other for *imbalance*.)

It's Not Just About Me
Form groups of three and read Romans 15:1-6 again. What does this passage teach you about balance? Do you tend to compartmentalize your internal life and your behavior, or do you see yourself as an integrated person, as the Jews? Explain.

How does the way you either fragment or integrate the various aspects of your self affect the way you live and behave in community? Where does your faith fit in?

If we view balance as having our mind, body, spirit, and emotions all receiving the attention they need, is balance a reasonable goal for you personally? Why or why not? Now extend this view of balance from the personal to the global level. Is personal balance on a global scale a reasonable goal? Why or why not? What is your vision of global balance? What do you imagine God's image of global balance to be?

IT'S NOT JUST ABOUT "ME"

Read Romans 15:1-6. This passage is part of a letter that Paul, a Christian convert and zealous missionary, wrote to the fledgling church in Rome. In Paul's time, Roman culture was greatly influenced by Greek philosophy, which emphasized individualism and personal well-being. Status was important in determining one's position in the society, and egalitarianism was a foreign concept. It was in this environment that Paul exhorted the early Roman Christians not to please themselves, but instead to put up with the weak and build up their neighbors. Paul's emphasis on caring community was definitely a radical idea.

Paul's words to the Romans teach us that while our own wellness is important, balance and wholeness mean much more than just personal health and well-being. Christian balance plays itself out in all our relationships. These include not only our relationships with those closest to us—spouse or significant other, parents, siblings, children, friends, employers, colleagues, and fellow church members—but also our sisters and brothers throughout the world whom we have never even met.

Although ancient Greek and Roman philosophy tended to compartmentalize the different aspects of an individual, the unity of mind, body, and spirit was an important concept in Jewish culture. This holistic view of self carried through into Christianity, and has significant implications for living a balanced life as a Christian. In personal balance, all the important facets of our life (mind, emotions, body, and spirit) receive the attention they need. Similarly, in the global concept of balance, everyone should have the opportunity to satisfy these same basic needs. In this broader context, we see that the vision of balance God intends for the world requires a commitment to justice and righteousness for all people and all of creation.

What must we balance to achieve the wholeness and abundance that God desires for the world? And how do we go about doing it? We may have a vision of where we want to go, but we have no idea how to get there. One thing is certain: A more balanced lifestyle requires change, which is often easier said than done. However, simply assessing our lives and recognizing that we need more balance is an important first step toward attaining it.

Balance and Imbalance

Read all three Gospel versions of Jesus' encounter with the rich young man (Matthew 19:16-30; Mark 10:17-31; and Luke 18:18-30.) What differences do you see in these accounts? We are never told how the story ends. Imagine yourself as the rich man in the story. What do you think happened to you after you left Jesus? What were your options? Which would you choose, and why? Finish the story in your own words, and share your ending with the rest of the group.

IS YOUR LIFE IN BALANCE?

How balanced is your life? Rate your lifestyle using the questions below.

A D (A = Agree, D = Disagree)

__ __ I wish I had more time for myself.

__ __ I wish I had more time with my family and friends.

__ __ It seems like my life is all work and no play.

__ __ My work is so stressful that it's taking a toll on my health.

__ __ Sometimes pursuing my desires gets me into trouble.

__ __ I should take better care of my body, but I don't have time.

__ __ I'm too busy (or tired) to go to church.

__ __ I'd like to have a closer relationship with God, but I just can't seem to set aside time to pray.

Form small groups and have each small group study a different Bible passage from the options given at the end of the Biblical Studies 101 box. Read enough of the story preceding the given verse to gain an understanding of its context. How could each verse be interpreted as advocating an unbalanced or extreme course of action? Could this apparent imbalance eventually result in a more balanced world? If so, how?

Is Your Life in Balance?
Form groups of three. If you are comfortable doing so, share the results of your balance self-assessment. Is there at least one aspect of your life where you feel you have it together? What facet of your life needs the most work to attain balance? What Christian values or Bible teachings influence either your current situation or your goals as they relate to balance? Close your sharing with silent prayer for each other, thanking God for the balance already attained and asking for guidance as you continue to strive for greater balance.

— — I don't feel like my partner and I contribute equally to our relationship.

— — Even though I'm really busy, it's hard to say no.

— — Sometimes I'm afraid to stand up for what's right.

— — I don't think I'm doing enough to make the world a better place.

Count the "agrees." If you score . . .

0   You're either really together or super-human.

1–4   What's your secret? Share it with the rest of us—then apply it to your remaining balance issues.

5–8   You're off to a good start, but there's plenty of room for growth. Keep trying!

9–12   You have some serious work to do, but join the club—it's a cultural phenomenon.

What's God Got to Do With It?
Read Psalm 127:1-2 again. Describe a time when you or someone you know put forth a great deal of effort to accomplish something, only to fail because God was left out of the picture. If the situation you describe is from your own experience, what would you do differently if you had the opportunity to try again? Now read Psalm 16, another psalm that provides some insight about balance. What does Psalm 16 tell you about balance and God's role in your quest for balance? Rewrite this psalm in your own words.

WHAT'S GOD GOT TO DO WITH IT?

At first glance, we might wonder how balance and our faith are related. After all, balance and associated issues such as stress reduction, time management, and priority setting are hot topics in the secular media and the business world. We may be led to believe that balance issues are best dealt with through psychology and self-discipline, and have little to do with our faith.

A truly balanced life, however, is more than a self-help project. Read Psalm 127:1-2. This psalm focuses on our dependence upon God for even the most basic provisions in everyday life. Psalm 127 may have been used on religious pilgrimages or at celebrations of the birth of a child to give instruction about leading a godly life. The first two verses teach us that without God at the center of our lives, all of our hard work is in vain. Applied to our discussion, we may recognize our need for balance and make a commitment to change our lives, but if we leave God out of the picture, our efforts are likely to fail. Without a relationship with God, we will never find true balance or experience the abundant life God intended.

BOTH/AND VS. EITHER/OR

One of the peculiarities of American culture is that we tend toward an "either/or" approach to life. A common illustration is the statement "I can either have a career or a family, but not both." When either/or thinking guides our decisions, we feel we must choose from mutually exclusive options. If one need wins, another must lose. This is particularly true when we try to manage our busy schedules. In the opening dialogue, for example, Sam took an either/or approach to finding time to attend church in the midst of his other commitments, and church lost out.

Our tendency toward polarized thinking contributes to our lack of balance, because it causes us to view the various demands on our time and energy as competing rather than complementary. The problem is further complicated by the fact that most, if not all, of those demands are worthwhile. Our decisions become more difficult when we choose between good and good rather than good and bad.

Sometimes our circumstances are dictated for us and we have little choice in how we use our time and energy. In other cases, however, the either/or choices we set up for

Look Closer
The last line of Psalm 16 refers to the fullness of joy we will find if we live in God's presence and follow God's guidance. Look up the words *fullness*, *joy*, and *abundance* in a Bible dictionary. How does Psalm 16:11 relate to the concept of abundance as Jesus explained it in John 10:10b? Using a concordance, look for these terms elsewhere in the Bible. Do you see any connections? How do they relate to your concept of a balanced life that relies on God?

Both/And Vs. Either/Or
Examine your own life as a case study. Think of an example of one "both/and" that you have already incorporated into your lifestyle. What different needs does this activity satisfy? How does it contribute to balance in your life? Now, think of an example of an "either/or" situation in your own life. How does your current approach to the situation limit your options? How might your faith lead you to look at the situation differently? Has God shown you any new "both/and" options to consider? If so, what are they, and how might they lead to greater balance in your life? Share your insights in small groups of three or four. Discuss how your shared experiences might help you find greater balance.

Your Challenge

Take a few minutes of silence to examine the images of your life. What is out of balance? What do you need to remove from your life? What might you need to add? Pledge to change one thing in your life this week as your first small step toward a more balanced lifestyle. Write down your pledge (perhaps in a prayer journal) and record any insights you gain throughout the week as you carry it out. If you wish, share your pledge for the coming week with the rest of the group.

Close with a group prayer. Start by having one person (perhaps the group facilitator) thank God for the time together to work on balance issues. Then take some time for individual silent reflection on any insights gained during the session and your pledge for the coming week. Close by having one person pray for insight and perseverance in the time until the next session, as you put your pledge into action and strive for greater balance.

ourselves are artificial. If we try instead to approach the problem of balance with the goal of finding "both/and" solutions, balance may be a little easier to attain. A both/and solution does not mean simply cramming more activity into our already busy schedules. Instead, it means looking for creative ways to structure our lives so that the activities we engage in satisfy different needs at the same time. It also means exploring a whole range of other options that we may never have considered.

A both/and approach to life will help us to take care of business while still enjoying the wholeness and abundance God intended for us. In each of the remaining chapters in this book, we will explore some specific both/and approaches to various issues related to balance.

YOUR CHALLENGE

Koyaanisqatsi, a Hopi Indian word meaning "life out of balance," was a popular art film in the 1980's. The film had no dialogue—just a series of images of beautiful nature scenes juxtaposed with images of environmental devastation and frenzied human activity.

Examine the images of your life. Do you live a "life out of balance?" Do you strive for greater balance? If so, a good place to start may be to focus on your relationship with God and seek God's guidance.

How can we cultivate a meaningful relationship with God? It is both easy and hard. Easy, because as Luke 11:9-10 tells us, if we want a relationship with God, all we have to do is ask. But hard because, as with any relationship, it takes time, effort, and clear intention. Challenge yourself now to take your first step toward a more balanced lifestyle by entering or strengthening your relationship with God.

I'M SO BUSY!

> This session will examine our need to establish healthy priorities that promote a more balanced life.

GETTING STARTED

Rachel: I quit my job so I could spend more time with my family and do volunteer work. But now I feel more busy and stressed than ever. Every time someone asks me to do something at church, I say yes, so people ask me all the time. Then later I regret it. I guess I should learn to say no, but I feel selfish turning them down.

Colleen: I love my job, and I'm quite successful, but it definitely controls my life. On a recent vacation, my husband and kids had fun at the beach while I was holed up in our hotel room with the phone, fax, and computer. Even when I joined them, I took along my pager because my clients need constant access. Sometimes I wonder if it's all worth it.

Joel: I wish I had your problems. I'm trying to raise three kids by myself, and I haven't ever taken a vacation. I'm so busy paying the bills, arranging for child care, and being both mom and dad to my kids that it makes my head

START
Greet one another and welcome newcomers. If you are comfortable doing so, briefly share your experiences of carrying out your pledge (from Session 1) to take a first step toward a more balanced lifestyle.

CASE STUDY
Can you identify with any of the people in the opening dialogue? If so, how? Can you think of any other profiles of over-busy people? Do you have an example from your own life to share? In each case, what is the source of the stress? What could each person (or you, if you are sharing your own example) do to find greater balance?

Time Crunch

Perform a time audit of your life. How much time do you spend in a typical day on your various activities? Draw the results in a pie graph, and share your findings in groups of three or four. Is the way you allocate your time an accurate indication of your priorities? How much time is under your control? How much is not? What do you wish you could spend less time doing? What would you do with more time if you had it? What do you consider "wasted time?"

DISCUSS

How do you feel about the pace of your life? In your mind's eye, visualize an image that represents your pace of life. Take a few minutes to express your image in a drawing, clay sculpture, collage, or other art form. (Have fun with this activity—you need not be artistic to do this.) When everyone is finished, display your artwork and explain what it means to the rest of the group.

spin. I'd like to be more involved in some of the civic organizations in my community, but there's no way. I'm afraid that if I stop to catch my breath, everything will fall apart.

Tom: Until recently, I ran a large homeless shelter in Chicago. All my life, I thought this was what God wanted me to do. But the pressures of the job never stopped. I was so busy running the program and dealing with crises that I never had time to establish relationships with the people I was supposed to be serving. I eventually became so burned out I left.

TIME CRUNCH

Our culture thrives on constant activity. For some, overbooked calendars have become status symbols as they rush from one activity to another. Others lack the luxury of filling their schedules with options, but are equally busy just trying to make ends meet. Working hours are increasing, and overtime and moonlighting have reached record highs. Regardless of our place on the economic ladder, time seems to be as scarce a resource as money.

Some of us may have over-busy lives in an attempt to "have it all." Some of us may be too busy out of necessity. In either case, we risk becoming so stressed and overtired that we lose any sense of satisfaction or fulfillment.

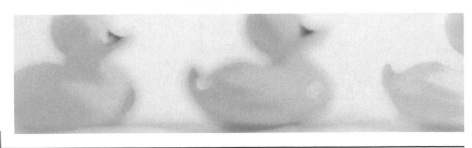

WHAT'S MISSING?

In our scramble to keep up with the demands of our calendars, are we missing something? We may think of over-busyness as unique to our modern culture, but in fact, the phenomenon has been around for at least two thousand years.

Read Luke 14:15-24. In this parable, an important host invited many people to an elaborate banquet. However, at the last minute, the invited guests made all kinds of excuses not to attend. They considered their worldly commitments more important than accepting the invitation to share in the feast.

Now read Luke 10:38-42, which relates the story of Jesus' visit to the home of his friends Mary and Martha. Martha, who busied herself with the necessary preparations for serving an honored guest, complained to Jesus about her sister Mary, who chose to sit and listen to Jesus. But Jesus gently told Martha that Mary had made the right decision.

What did the invited dinner guests (Luke 14:15-24) and Martha (Luke 10:38-42) miss when they chose to put business first? What is the point of these two stories? What do they tell us about prioritizing our lives?

WHERE ARE YOUR PRIORITIES?

Read Matthew 6:19-21.

Imagine yourself as one of Jesus' disciples in first-century Palestine. Not long ago, you were minding your own business, making a modest living as a fisherman on the Sea of Galilee. Then Jesus came along and began preaching in the nearby synagogues about

What's Missing?
Read Luke 14:15-24 again. What excuses did the invited guests make to get out of attending the banquet? Retell or rewrite the story in a contemporary setting, from your own experience if possible. In pairs, share your modern version of the story. What invitation was made? What excuses were given for turning it down? What were the consequences of declining the invitation? If your story is based on your own experience, would you choose a different outcome now? Why?

Read Luke 10:38-42 again. Have three volunteers act out the roles of Jesus, Mary, and Martha as a "fishbowl exercise," with the rest of the group as onlookers. Then, as a group, discuss the experience. What do you think about the choices Mary and Martha made? What would you have done in their shoes? Do you think Martha felt like she had a choice? Have you ever experienced a situation like that of Mary and Martha? What were your options, and which did you choose? Did you miss something wonderful or "choose the better part?"

Where Are Your Priorities?

Make two columns on a blank sheet of paper. In the left column, list the top five priorities in your life in order of importance, starting with the highest. In the right column, list in order your five most time-consuming activities. (Refer to your time audit if you made one earlier in the session.) Then draw lines between the columns to match your priorities with your time use. How do the two columns correspond? Does the way you spend your time agree with your priorities? If not, why not? Look back to Matthew 6:21, substituting the word *time* for *treasure*. Is it true that where your time is, so your heart is also? If not, what could you change? Share your results in pairs.

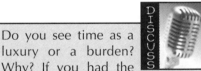

Do you see time as a luxury or a burden? Why? If you had the choice, would you give up time to make more money, or give up money to make more time? What would you have to sacrifice in your life to make such a change? What would you gain?

the kingdom of heaven. One day, out of the blue, Jesus came to you while you were working and called you to leave everything behind and follow him. What a radical command! After all, how would you survive if you abandoned your livelihood? However, you obeyed, and ever since, you have accompanied him throughout the region as he preached, taught, and healed. But you still don't understand what it really means to be his disciple.

One day, weary from the constant traveling and exhausted by the demands of the crowds, Jesus leads you and the other disciples up a hillside for some quiet rest. As you settle back, Jesus finally starts to teach you about what it means to follow him and live according to the will of God.

Eventually, Jesus comes to a subject of great concern to you in your newly-unemployed state: money. He exhorts you not to spend your efforts accumulating material possessions that have no lasting value, but instead to focus on the spiritual wealth that comes from serving God.

Today, we call Jesus' instructions for living a godly life, the "Sermon on the Mount" (Matthew 5–7). While Matthew 6:19-21 is about money or possessions, in a broader sense it also addresses the priorities we set in our lives. In our contemporary context, this passage has something to teach us about time as well. Read Matthew 6:21 again, this time substituting the word *time* for *treasure*. Does the resulting phrase have any meaning for you? Is it true that where your time is, your heart will be also? What are the implications of this verse for the way you prioritize your time?

PERMISSION TO REST

In our culture, many of us learn from a young age to worship industriousness. Productivity is one of our nation's most important economic indicators, and rest and play are considered unproductive. Religious tradition has reinforced this view with sayings like "The devil finds work for idle hands." While a strong work ethic can certainly have a very positive influence on our lives, when taken to the extreme it can be unhealthy if we do not give ourselves permission to rest. Wayne Muller, an ordained minister and advocate for social justice, suggests that the over-busyness that accompanies a so-called "successful" life is actually a form of violence that hurts our bodies, our spirits, our relationships, and the earth on which we depend.

While certain Scripture passages such as Proverbs 6:6-11 and 19:15 warn against idleness, the Bible emphasizes that God's rest is good. Jesus stated this explicitly in Matthew 11:28-30, when he said, "Come to me, all you that are weary and are carrying heavy burdens, and I will give you rest." On many occasions during his ministry, Jesus demonstrated the importance of rest by leaving the crowds to pray and renew himself in solitude.

God not only gives us permission to rest, but commands us to do so in the fourth commandment: "Remember the sabbath day, and keep it holy." Read Exodus 20:8-11. As God described it to Moses, sabbath requires one day a week of rest for ourselves and anyone we employ, during which time we are to refrain from all forms of work and to consecrate the day to God.

Permission to Rest
Read Proverbs 6:6-11 and Matthew 11:28-30. What is the difference between laziness and rest? Are the two ever confused in our culture? If so, how? Do you give yourself permission to rest? To play? What happens to your mind, body, spirit, and relationships when you have inadequate rest?

Read Exodus 20:8-10 again. What does sabbath mean to you? Is the concept relevant anymore? What do you think is the purpose of sabbath? How (if at all) did you practice sabbath in your childhood? If not, why not? How has your practice of sabbath changed in your adult life? Why? Is your faith leading you to practice sabbath differently?

Psalms 23 and 131 both evoke images of rest as a gift from God. Read one of these psalms. How does it make you feel? What does it mean to rest in God? Do you have any personal experience of God's rest? Write down your thoughts about the psalm you chose. You may wish to rewrite the psalm in your own words.

LOOK CLOSER

How did Jesus observe the sabbath? How did he respond to the rules and regulations associated with sabbath? Form three small groups and have each choose a different Scripture passage: Luke 13:10-17; Matthew 12:9-14; or Mark 2:23-28. Using a Bible commentary, look up the background material explaining your passage. Why was Jesus accused of violating the sabbath? Who criticized him? How did Jesus respond to the accusations? What are the implications of Jesus' actions for the way we keep sabbath today? What rules, if any, are appropriate for observing the sabbath today? Share your findings with the whole group.

CASE STUDY

Can Christians Say No?

Look back to the four people in the opening dialogue. How do you think the issue of saying no plays into each situation? How free do they seem to say no, and what would be the consequences of their doing so? Using your own life as a case study, think of a time when you overextended yourself because you did not want to say no. Or, think of a time when you had to say no, but felt guilty about it. Was your decision based on God's leading or other factors? What were the consequences of your choice? What role does your faith play in your decisions about your time? What can you do to discern God's will in establishing your priorities?

Christian practice for observing the sabbath has undergone tremendous change over the past few generations. In our great-grandparents' time, most businesses were closed on Sundays, and sabbath for many Christians consisted of going to church and resting. Today our economy operates 24 hours a day, seven days a week, and many work schedules no longer accommodate Sundays off. An endless variety of leisure activities, many of which require the labor of others, are available to occupy our non-working hours. Is the concept of sabbath even relevant anymore? If so, how can we find time to keep it, and what does it mean to do so?

CAN CHRISTIANS SAY NO?

An important step on the road to balance may be learning to say no. Of course, for some people, saying no is not an option, especially on the job. Still, like Rachel in the opening dialogue, many Christians have trouble with this small word, especially when asked to do "good things" for the church or other people. Unfortunately, spreading ourselves too thin, even for a good cause, can lead to resentment, burnout, and damaged relationships.

Our reluctance to say no when given the choice may stem from guilt at the thought

32

of turning our backs on a legitimate need. Or, it may stem from an inflated view of our own importance. We may sometimes think the project will fail if we do not personally see to every detail. Perhaps we do not trust God to take over when we need rest.

Jesus' words in Matthew 5:33-37 indicate that at times it is all right to say no, as long as we speak the truth plainly. To be effective servants, we need to establish our priorities and focus our efforts in the areas where God really calls us to serve.

Getting Off the Wheel
Take a few minutes to brainstorm ways to make sabbath time in your life. Then list some important things in your life that you wish you had more time for. Apply the "both/and" approach to your two lists. How could you use your sabbath time to fulfill aspects of your life that need more attention? How do you think God wants you to use your sabbath time?

GETTING OFF THE WHEEL

How can we find time for rest and renewal in the midst of our busy schedules? How can we obey God's commandment to keep the sabbath when we are already so overloaded? One way may be to apply the "both/and" approach that we discussed in Session 1. What, besides rest, is short-

Biblical Studies 101: *Sabbath Rest*

The importance placed on sabbath rest in Scripture is clear. Sabbath is one of the first three concepts presented in the Bible. The Book of Genesis starts out by telling us that God exists, God created everything, and then God rested. The directive to observe the sabbath is fourth among the Ten Commandments. Why does God insist that we keep the sabbath? Two reasons are given in biblical descriptions of the Ten Commandments. The first, according to Exodus 20:8-11, is because the sabbath is holy. Genesis 2:3 tells us that God blessed the sabbath and made it holy because it was the day God rested from the work of Creation. The second reason is because keeping the sabbath is an act of justice. Deuteronomy 5:12-15 commands us to observe the sabbath to remember that God saved the Israelites from slavery and oppression. Therefore, we should treat others (and ourselves) justly by providing regular opportunities for sabbath rest. In what ways do these two biblical justifications for observing the sabbath relate to balance?

I'm So Busy!

Several hymns have been written about the peace that comes from resting in God. Sing or recite together one or more of the following hymns: "Come and Find the Quiet Center," "Serenity," "Take Time to Be Holy," "Near to the Heart of God," or "Not So in Haste, My Heart." What feelings do these hymns evoke in you? What does it mean to "take time to be holy?" How could you use your sabbath time to put the words of these hymns into practice?

SMALL GROUP

Your Challenge

If you wish, share your pledge for the coming week with the rest of the group. Then observe a five-minute period of silent "mini-sabbath." Use this time in a way that would be meaningful to you. (Not everyone need do the same thing.) For example, you might use the time to pray, read, and reflect on Scripture (try Ecclesiastes 3:1-8), write in a journal, sketch a picture, or simply be still and rest.

CLOSE

As a group, close with a circle prayer. Anyone wishing to pray aloud about issues related to time and balance may do so, but everyone should be welcome to pass. Begin your prayer time by thanking God for the gift of sabbath. End by praying for God's guidance as you put your pledge into practice.

changed in your life? Perhaps it is relaxed time with family and friends, or a chance to enjoy nature, or attention to physical exercise, or time alone with God in prayer.

Think of ways to spend your sabbath time that would help you meet the needs you just identified. You can do this even if your sabbath only consists of minutes a week instead of a whole day. Try taking a five-minute sabbath during a busy work day to stroll by a flower bed, chat with a friend, or read a daily devotional. Even a 30-second sabbath for some quiet reflection in an empty rest room is better than none at all. If we view sabbath not as wasted time, but rather as a precious opportunity to attend to areas of our lives that can bring us joy and fulfillment, we are more likely to find time to observe it.

YOUR CHALLENGE

The saying "all work and no play makes Jack a dull boy" describes an unfortunate consequence of our over-busy culture. In Christian terms, we can say that too much busyness makes us miss the abundance and joy God intended for us.

Are you overloaded? What is missing in your life because of your busyness? What part of your busyness is least necessary? Is any of it self-imposed? Even if you are over-busy by necessity instead of choice, there is probably something you can do to create some stillness in your life, if only for a few minutes a day. Make a pledge (and write it down) to set aside time and space in your life this week for some form of sabbath rest.

WHAT A RUSH!

> This session will explore the balance between meeting our everyday responsibilities and pushing the limits to satisfy our need for fun, excitement, and adventure.

GETTING STARTED

Felicia: I used to dream of all the exciting things I'd do after college. I planned to travel, meet fascinating people, make an important contribution to society and serve God in exciting ways. But now I'm in a rut. I spend all my time meeting my routine obligations, and I'm not really going anywhere. What happened?

Ellie: Sometimes it seems like I'm living in two separate worlds, and it's hard to know how they fit together. I take my faith seriously, but I also like to have a good time. When I go out and party with my friends on Saturday night, and then turn around and go to church on Sunday morning, I feel like a hypocrite. My life isn't balanced when I feel like two different people.

Steve: Balance? Sorry, that sounds a little too tame for me. I work hard so I can play hard. My folks keep telling me it's time to settle down and start acting my age, but why should I? The last thing I want is a boring life with nothing to look forward to.

START

Greet one another and welcome newcomers. If you are comfortable doing so, briefly share your experiences of carrying out your pledge (from Session 2) to set aside time and space for sabbath rest.

CASE STUDY

Can you identify with any of the people in the "Getting Started" section? If so, how? Share your own example of a time when you had to balance your responsibilities with your need for fun and excitement. How did you resolve the situation?

Growing Up, Settling Down

In a hallway or clear space, make a long line on the floor with masking tape. Label one end "settled and responsible" and the other end "unsettled and adventurous." Stand on the line in a place that represents (1) your current situation; then (2) where you would like to be; and finally (3) where you think God wants you to be. After the exercise, discuss the results. Where on the continuum can balance be found? Is this place different for others than it is for you? What are the differences between where you are, where you want to be, and where God wants you to be? What might you need to change in your life to find a more balanced position?

SMALL GROUP

Form groups of three or four and talk about the following questions. How can too much excitement be unhealthy? How can too little excitement be as harmful as too much? As Christians, should we always avoid extreme behavior, or is it desirable in some situations?

Mitch: I feel like my life is pretty tame compared to most people I know. I've never really walked on the wild side and don't have any burning desire to start now. My life is full, and I'm happy. Still, I get the impression that if I'm not living on the edge, I'm somehow missing all that life has to offer. Am I wrong to not want more? Does God expect more from me?

Suzanne: Living on the edge isn't all it's cracked up to be. Just living in my neighborhood is an adventure and not a pleasant one. I hear all this talk about bored people wanting more excitement in their lives. But I long for just the opposite—safety and tranquillity—and I'll probably never get it.

GROWING UP, SETTLING DOWN

Not long ago, the expected pattern of adult life in our culture was to finish school, get a job, get married, and have children. Early adulthood was a time to go a little wild, but once that was over it was time to grow up and settle down. Today, because of recent social changes including later marriages, better jobs at earlier ages for many people, and mass media that idolize adventure, settling down may seem less attractive. Our culture tells us that settling down is boring, and it encourages us instead to seek excitement and satisfy all our desires.

As Christians in a society that values the relentless pursuit of pleasure for its own sake, how are we to behave? Is it possible to find balance between living a responsible life and having enough excitement to keep life interesting?

Read Ecclesiastes 2:1-11. Ecclesiastes is an example of Old Testament Wisdom literature written to teach people about moral conduct. Taken alone, the point of this passage seems clear: The pursuit of pleasure for its own sake is meaningless vanity, from which nothing good can be gained. The tone of the text can sound quite negative. In fact, the whole book of Ecclesiastes could easily be described as reflections of a grumpy old man.

Reading more of Ecclesiastes helps put these verses in perspective. For example, Ecclesiastes 2:18-23 tells us our hard work is meaningless, too, and 1:12-18 implies that even the pursuit of wisdom is an exercise in futility. The negativity seems overwhelming, but further study shows a positive message about balance.

Read Ecclesiastes 2:24-25; 3:10-13; and 5:18-20. These passages teach that we *can* enjoy our pleasures and work, as long as we recognize that the joy we find in them is a gift from God. In other words, God is the source of our satisfaction, not the pleasure or work we pursue. Placing God at the focal point of our activities will help us keep them in balance and prevent excesses that may lead to unhealthy ends.

WHO AM I REALLY?

When we fail to focus on God in all our activities, we run the risk of leading fragmented lives that separate our spirituality from our everyday behavior and leave us wondering who we really are. Remember Ellie from the opening dialogue? Although her faith was important to her, she compartmentalized the spiritual component of her life. Ellie expressed doubt about the compatibility of her Saturday-night behavior and her Sunday-morning faith. This left her feeling confused, unsatisfied, and out of balance.

LOOK CLOSER

Read Ecclesiastes 1:12-18; 2:1-11; 2:18-23; 2:24-25; 3:10-13; and 5:18-20 again. Then, using a Bible commentary, look up background information on Ecclesiastes and interpretations of the passages you just read. (You may choose to form small groups and assign one or two passages to each person.) What is the overall theme of Ecclesiastes? How does it relate to balance? Does the tone seem negative to you? If so, why? Do you find any positive messages in the passages you read? How could practicing these teachings help you attain greater balance?

CASE STUDY

Who Am I Really?
Look again at Ellie's statement in the opening dialogue. How could Ellie bring the two aspects of herself together to find balance and wholeness? Is feeling like different people in different situations a normal part of life, or does it represent fragmentation that could have unhealthy consequences? Have you ever experienced situations where you felt that your actions were incompatible with your faith? What did you do about the conflict? How did your faith influence your response?

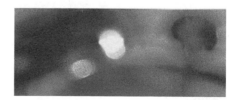

What a Rush!

Read and reflect silently on Richard Foster's quote about "inner apartheid." Do you think this quote describes you? If so, how do you compartmentalize the spiritual part of your life? How does this fragmentation affect you, and how might you overcome it? If not, how have you integrated your spiritual life into your everyday activities? What effect has this integration had on your life? Write down your insights, perhaps in a prayer journal. If you are comfortable doing so, share your reflections with two or three others.

What Are the Rules?

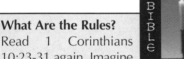

Read 1 Corinthians 10:23-31 again. Imagine yourself as a member of the early Corinthian church who has just read Paul's letter. Remember that converting to Christianity itself was for Gentiles a very isolating act. How would you interpret Paul's teaching in this passage, and how would you respond? In your own life, what does it mean to "do everything for the glory of God?" How should this directive influence the choices you make about your everyday activities and behavior?

According to Richard Foster, author of *Prayer: Finding the Heart's True Home* (Harper San Francisco, 1992), situations like Ellie's are common. Foster aptly described the condition as "a kind of inner apartheid. We segregate out a small corner of pious activities and then can make no spiritual sense out of the rest of our lives. We have become so accustomed to this way of living that we fail to see the contradiction in it. The scandal of Christianity in our day is the heresy of a 5 percent spirituality."

WHAT ARE THE RULES?

We can restore balance and wholeness to our fragmented selves by allowing our spirituality to permeate our entire lives. Ideally, our faith will influence everything we do. But how can we know if our behavior is compatible with our faith? Is it possible to live a Christian life and have fun doing it? What are the rules, and to what extent must we adhere to them?

Some of the first Christians struggled with similar questions. Read 1 Corinthians 10:23-31. Paul wrote these words in a letter to the early church in Corinth, a Roman-controlled city in southern Greece. This passage was written in response to the Corinthian Christians' confusion about whether they, as Gentile (non-Jewish) converts, needed to observe Jewish dietary laws. Strict adherence to these laws would prevent the church members from eating in the homes of their unbelieving friends. Paul advised the church that it was not necessary to follow the Jewish laws regarding food. However, he was emphatic that they must do nothing to offend other believers, and encouraged them to do everything, even eating and drinking, for the glory of God.

It seems that in this case Paul was relatively unconcerned about specific do's and don'ts, as long as the church members' actions glorified God. Think again about Ellie. If Paul were alive today, do you think he would give her the same advice he gave to the Corinthians?

DOES BALANCE MEAN BORING?

Read Proverbs 4:25-27, another example of wisdom literature. What image do these proverbs bring to mind? We often hear that the road to faith is "a straight and narrow path." The concept of balance is commonly associated with the phrase "do everything in moderation." While these statements may be very good advice, let's face it: they sound a little bland. Many of us are turned off by exhortations to lead a more balanced life because we associate balance with boredom.

The Bible, however, tells us differently. There are many stories of godly people in the Bible whose lives were anything but dull! Jesus is a prime example. As a child, Jesus fled with his family to Egypt to escape persecution and death. As an adult, Jesus was in contact with people from every station in life, from rulers to prostitutes, and that was often a source of conflict. He began his ministry with a solitary forty-day trek in the desert with no food. He ended it with a triumphal march into Jerusalem, followed by imprisonment, death, and resurrection. In between, he traveled by foot and boat in the course of his ministry, dependent on God and other people for his day-to-day sustenance.

Today, we have many role models of Christians who lead exciting lives while

Does Balance Mean Boring?

Place two signs in opposite corners of your meeting room, one labeled "yes" and the other "no." Reflect on what you know about Jesus. Do you think Jesus lived a balanced life? (Move to the corner of the room corresponding to your choice.) In the group you chose, discuss why you chose the answer you did. If you answered yes, in what ways was Jesus' life a model of balance? How do you think Jesus was able to attain balance in the midst of the difficult circumstances of his life? If you answered no, in what ways did Jesus live an unbalanced life? Do you think Jesus intended to live a balanced life? If Jesus could not attain balance, are our attempts to do so futile? When finished, share your insights with the other group. What lessons about balance can we learn from studying the life of Jesus?

LOOK CLOSER

Think of other role models at the cutting edge of life and Christian service. Who are they? What do they do, and why do they do it? Do you think their lives are balanced? Have you ever dreamed of engaging in some type of service or action outside of your comfort zone? If so, what is it? How difficult would it be for you to make your dream a reality? What would you have to give up in order to do so? Within the constraints of your current circumstances, what are some feasible ways you could serve God and others outside of your comfort zone?

Paul's Life of Adventure

Form four groups, each to read a different one of the following passages from Acts: 9:1-19a; 9:19b-25; 16:16-34; and 27:1-28:6. Recount the events of the story. How did Paul end up in such a dangerous or dramatic situation? Do you think Paul was an adventure addict, a victim of circumstances, or something else? Could he have accomplished his ministry in less exciting and dangerous ways? Share your findings with the other groups. Do you think Paul led a balanced life? Why or why not?

Biblical Studies 101: *Paul's Life of Adventure*

The Apostle Paul was another biblical figure whose life personified adventure. Acts 9:1-19 tells the story of Paul's dramatic conversion to Christianity. A Pharisee who devoutly upheld Jewish law, Paul persecuted Christians until he met the resurrected Christ on the road to Damascus. A zealous missionary after his conversion, Paul's efforts to spread the news about Jesus and start new churches involved widespread travel. In the course of his ministry, Paul was jailed and threatened with death numerous times. Once, he escaped death when his friends hid him in a basket and lowered him over the Damascus city wall (Acts 9:19b-25). Later, when Paul was imprisoned in Philippi, a violent earthquake unlocked the prison doors and released his chains (Acts 16:16-34). Eventually, he was arrested in Jerusalem and transported by ship to Rome for trial. During the voyage, he and his fellow travelers were shipwrecked after a fierce two-week storm at sea. Taking refuge on the island of Malta, he was attacked by a venomous snake, and then revered as a god when he did not die (Acts 27:1-28:6). Clearly, Paul's passion for Christ led him to life on the edge.

serving at the cutting edge of ministry. Examples from recent history include Dr. Martin Luther King, Jr., Mother Teresa, and Bishop Desmond Tutu. Thousands of less famous and unknown people find balance and fulfillment while serving in homeless shelters, refugee camps, and other situations far outside their comfort zones.

Balance does not have to be boring. In fact, one result of a more balanced life can be the alleviation of boredom. A truly balanced life exposes us to a variety of people and experiences, freeing us from dull routine. When we open ourselves to God's leading, doors open and exciting opportunities arise that we never thought possible.

THOU SHALT NOT—?

Some of us learned in childhood that Christianity is all about don'ts. For some, living a faithful life is defined more by what they cannot do than what they can. Certainly, the Bible contains some very important prohibitions that are essential to our faith, starting with eight of the Ten Commandments (Exodus 20:1-17). However, focusing exclusively on prohibitions may cause us to miss the most important part of the Bible's message. Taken as a whole, the Bible is much more about do's than don'ts, and the do's present far greater opportunity for challenge and adventure.

Balance: Living With Life's Demands

Read Matthew 19:16-22; 22:34-40; 25:31-46; and 28:16-20. These biblical do's, which Jesus taught and exemplified in his own life, represented a radical departure from the cultural values of Jesus' time. They are just as important and radical today, and if we truly lived according to these teachings, our lives and faith would be the ultimate adventure. For those of us brought up to think of Christianity as a litany of "thou shalt not's," focusing on the positive commandments in the Bible may empower us to practice our faith in a different and much more exciting way.

OUTWARD BOUND, GOD-STYLE

Read Luke 9:23. Jesus made this statement to his disciples after acknowledging to them that he was, indeed, the Messiah. He then warned them that he would suffer and be killed, and told them that to be his followers, they must "take up their cross daily" and follow him.

What does Luke 9:23 mean to us as followers of Christ today? How are we to take up our cross daily? Some of us, like Suzanne and Mitch in the "Getting Started" section, may be perfectly happy living a peaceful life and serving God and others in quiet ways. Others need some adventure to feel fully alive. Both approaches are normal characteristics of our God-given personalities. In fact, a recent study by US and Israeli scientists suggests that our degree of thrill-seeking behavior has a genetic basis.

DISCUSS

Thou Shalt Not—?
List the don'ts that you associate with Christianity. Which don'ts are generally accepted among Christians and which are debated? Which ones have a biblical basis? Of those that don't, why do you think they are part of certain Christian traditions? How do you discern which prohibitions are important and which are just cultural habits? How do the "don'ts" of your faith tradition influence how you behave?

BIBLE

Form four groups, each to discuss a different one of the following passages from Matthew: 19:16-22; 22:34-40; 25:31-46; and 28:16-20. How do you think Jesus' audience understood these commandments at the time? How do you understand these commandments in the context of your own life? To what extent are you living out these commandments? If you took these commandments more seriously, how would they change your view of the Christian faith? How would they change your life?

BIBLE

Outward Bound
Read Luke 9:23 again. Reflect on the last time you made a choice to "take up your cross" and follow Christ. (Remember that this means something for which you would make a significant sacrifice as Jesus did, not just some annoyance.) Discuss what it means to "take up our cross daily." How often do you really take up the cross? What prevents you? Are the actions described large or small? What did you learn about following Jesus from sharing these experiences?

Do you have a natural inclination for adventure, or do you prefer a quieter lifestyle? How does the way you engage in ministry reflect your natural inclination? Who are your biblical role models for ministry? Do you think God calls all Christians to step out of their comfort zones? Why or why not? List as many ways as you can think of to serve in ministry outside of your comfort zone. Which ideas do you find most appealing? Why? How feasible are they for you?

God calls all of us to some form of ministry, not just clergy—we honor God and serve others in our everyday lives. Fortunately, ministry can be as exciting as we make it. For Christians with a need to live on the edge, our concept of both/and solutions may help us identify activities and careers that allow us to satisfy our desire for adventure while serving others in Christ's name. Mission work and volunteer vacations provide opportunities to travel, experience other cultures, and interact with a great variety of people through Christian service projects. Working with youth in Christian adventure camps may satisfy a desire to be outdoors and practice survival skills while helping young people grow in their faith. Serving in homeless shelters or refugee camps may help us put the concept of living on the edge in perspective. Opportunities for meaningful and exciting service are limitless if we are willing to leave our comfort zone.

SMALL GROUP

Your Challenge

Take a few minutes of silence to think about how God is calling you to ministry. What does ministry mean to you? What is your "comfort zone" for ministry? Is there a type of ministry that you would love to do, but you find the prospect too frightening to actually do it? If God gave you the courage and the means to engage in this ministry, how do you think your life would change? Pledge to spend time in prayer throughout the coming week to discern if and how God might be calling you to ministry outside of your comfort zone. Write down any insights you gain. If you wish, share your thoughts from your silent reflection with the rest of the group.

YOUR CHALLENGE

A popular Army recruitment slogan several years ago was "It's not just a job, it's an adventure!" Ideally, we ought to be able to say the same for our Christian faith. God does not want us to sleep through our lives, crossing off the days on the calendar. On the other hand, God does not want us to hurt ourselves in attempts to seek adventure for its own sake.

What scares you the most about following Christ? If you truly seek adventure, perhaps you should challenge yourself with your response to this question. Is God calling you to meet this challenge?

CLOSE

Close by praying aloud, if you wish, about your own call to ministry or struggle with balance may do so. Begin the prayer by asking God for a clearer vision of the ministry God desires for each person. End by praying for courage to engage in ministry in bold and creative ways.

O LORD, WHERE ARE YOU?

This session will explore how we can strengthen our relationship with God in the midst of our daily routine and, in doing so, lead a more balanced life.

GETTING STARTED

Ian: There have been a few exhilarating times in my life when I've felt really connected to God. Then that closeness goes away, and it's like it never happened. I'm a Christian, but lately I feel like I'm just going through the motions. How can I get that inspiration back?

Deanne: I know I should pray and read the Bible, but I just don't have time. I wish I could, but it's impossible. I can't keep up with all my responsibilities as it is—there's no way I can add anything more to my "to do" list.

Tyler: It's harder to have a devotional life now that I'm in college. There's no privacy, and my friends and roommates are definitely not into it. I get some funny looks when I head off to church on Sunday mornings. It's a little embarrassing to be a Christian, to be honest.

Dan: My life is as hectic as anyone else's. But when I take

START

Greet one another and welcome newcomers. If you are comfortable doing so, briefly share your experiences of carrying out your pledge (from Session 3) to discern how God might be calling you to serve outside of your comfort zone.

CASE STUDY

Can you identify with any of the people in the "Getting Started" section? If so, how? How would you assess each person's relationship with God? How do you think their relationship with God influences the degree of balance in their lives? What do you think might hinder their spiritual life? How might they overcome these barriers? If you are comfortable, share insights about your own relationship with God and how it affects other facets of your life.

BIBLE

Unsatisfied Longings
Read Psalm 42 again. In silence, think about a time when you may have experienced similar feelings of alienation from God or longing for God's presence. Then rewrite Psalm 42 in your own words, based on your own experience. Or, draw a picture that represents the feelings that Psalm 42 evokes in you. If you are comfortable doing so, share your psalm or drawing with the rest of the group. Was your longing for God ever satisfied? If so, how?

DISCUSS

If you can, recall a time when you felt close to God, or when you knew God was acting directly in your life. Describe the experience. What was your relationship with God like before this experience? After? Did the experience influence your devotional life in any way? If so, how? If you have never felt especially close to God, imagine what such an experience might be like and describe it. Do you long for such an experience? What are you willing to change in your life to draw closer to God? If you had a closer relationship with God, how do you think it would change you?

time to spend alone with God on a regular basis, everything in my life just seems to fall into place a little better. I'm less stressed out and more creative. My problems don't go away, but I seem to be able to deal with them better.

Jenna: I wanted so much to feel God's presence in my life. I followed the advice of my Christian friends, went to church each week, and prayed and studied every day. But God still felt so distant. Then I got roped into helping a friend who works at a women's shelter. I dreaded the experience, but once I got there I felt closer to God than I had in a long time. Maybe I needed to look outward, not just inward.

UNSATISFIED LONGINGS

Read Psalm 42. This psalm is a lament, a poem in which the author cries out for relationship with God. Psalm 42 was probably written by an Israelite living in exile who longed to worship God in the Jerusalem Temple in his faraway homeland. Jewish tradition held that God could only be worshiped properly in the Temple. The physical distance from Jerusalem made the writer feel alienated from and perhaps even forgotten by God.

Most of us, at some point in our lives, have probably experienced a similar longing for God. It is difficult to live a balanced life if we neglect our spiritual needs. Even if we are satisfied by our life and fulfilled by our faith, we may hunger for a deeper, more intimate relationship with God. Unfortunately, even though we earnestly desire it, sometimes our relationship with God takes a back seat to other demands that seem more obvious and immediate. Perhaps we fail to realize that a relationship with God requires diligence, time, and faithful effort on our part. Sometimes we give up too soon; at others, we do not know where to start.

WHAT IS A "DEVOTIONAL LIFE?"

Many of us have heard the phrase "devotional life" or know people who practice "daily devotions," but what does this mean? Often, the word *devotions* is used to describe the regular practice of setting aside time to spend alone with God. In a broader sense, devotional life refers to all the things we do to invite God to enter into and transform our lives. In this context, our devotional life includes both private (inward) and community (outward) experiences with God.

The first Christians provide an excellent model for a devotional life. Read Acts 2:37-47. This passage describes the activities of the first people to join the new Christian church on the day of Pentecost. Imagine the scene. After experiencing the devastation of Jesus' death on the cross and the astonishing joy of his resurrection three days later, Jesus' disciples had spent 40 days learning from the resurrected Christ. Jesus then ascended into heaven, promising his followers that he would send them the Holy Spirit. The Spirit came upon them at Pentecost (an annual Jewish festival that attracted Jews of many nationalities to Jerusalem) in the form of a violent wind and tongues of fire. Suddenly, the disciples gained the ability to speak of the wonders of God in many languages, astonishing the crowd. Peter preached to the multitude that Jesus was, indeed, God's Messiah. Three thousand people became

SMALL GROUP

What Is a "Devotional Life?"

In pairs, discuss your devotional life. Do you have a devotional life? If so, describe it. What is the place of the classical disciplines of prayer, study, worship, fellowship, and service in your life? Why (or why not) do you spend time on these spiritual disciplines? Are there other ways through which you experience God, such as the creative arts, tending plants, exercise and play, or other? What are they? How (if at all) do the disciplines you practice benefit you? How (if at all) do they benefit God? What, if anything, would you like to change about your devotional life? Why?

BIBLE

Read Acts 2:37-47 again. Do you think the biblical model of the Christian church described in Acts 2 is applicable today? Does God expect us to practice our faith in the same ways as the early Christians did? Why or why not? If you answered yes, how well do you think your churches and you are living up to God's expectations?

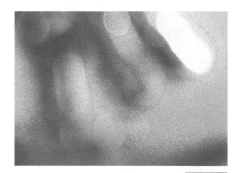

converts, marking the beginning of the Christian church.

But once converted, what were they to do? According to the Scripture, the new converts "devoted themselves to the apostles' teaching and fellowship, to the breaking of bread and the prayers." In addition, they praised God together, shared all their material possessions for the good of the community, and supported the apostles in their service and healing. These activities of the first Christians constitute the elements of devotional life that believers have practiced ever since: prayer, study, worship, fellowship, and service. Today, the same practices, sometimes called "spiritual disciplines," can help us to engage in a deeper, more intimate relationship with God.

PRAYER: QUALITY TIME WITH GOD

Read Matthew 6:5-15. In this part of the Sermon on the Mount, Jesus taught his disciples how to pray, using what we now call "The Lord's Prayer" as a model. Prayer, along with charitable giving and fasting, was one of the three principal spiritual disciplines of the Jewish faith in Jesus' time, and Jesus' teaching confirmed that it was a vital part of Christian practice as well.

Imagine trying to have a meaningful or intimate relationship with someone without ever having a conversation. Yet that is exactly what many of us do when we say we want a spiritual life but fail to spend time with God in prayer. An active prayer life will keep our whole life in balance, because it will help us to discern God's guidance in the midst of our many competing demands. A common flaw in our prayer lives is too much talk and not enough listening. In his book *Discipleship* (Plough Publishing House, 1994), J. Heinrich Arnold wrote, "In our prayer life we need to listen to the spirit of God. What God wants to tell us is of greater importance than what we want to tell him."

Many people who are new to prayer feel unsure about how to pray or where to begin. Others who grew up in the church may find that the ways they learned to pray as a child are no longer satisfying. Much has been written on methods of prayer, and there is no single "right" way to pray. If you want to enrich your prayer life, it may help to experiment with a number of methods. The most important thing is to find a quiet time and place and make prayer a regular habit.

STUDY: READ THE BOOK

One way God speaks to us is through the Scriptures. Read Romans 12:2. In this part of his letter to the Roman church, Paul exhorts his followers to "be transformed by the renewing of your minds." Clearly, a relationship with God is not purely an exercise of our hearts and emotions, but of our intellects as well. And one of the best ways to learn about God is by studying the Bible.

It is common for people new to the Bible to feel somewhat intimidated by it, especially if they attempt to read it cover to cover. However, there are numerous ways of studying the Bible that make it less daunting and more

LOOK CLOSER

Read Matthew 6:5-15. When Jesus taught his disciples to pray in this passage, do you think he intended for them (and us) to pray this exact prayer, or to use it as a model for our own prayers? Using biblical commentaries or other references, read some background material about this passage. Then analyze the Lord's Prayer line by line. How much of it is devoted to asking God for things? What does Jesus ask for? What other elements does Jesus model in this prayer (praise, thanksgiving, for example)? Compare the content of your own prayers with the Lord's prayer. Compared to Jesus' model, do you over- or under-emphasize anything when you pray?

SMALL GROUP

Study: Read the Book
In one corner of the room, place a sign on the wall that reads "I find the Bible frustrating and intimidating." In the opposite corner, place a sign that reads, "I find great joy and enrichment from reading the Bible." Move to the corner (not in between) that most closely corresponds to your own attitude about the Bible. In the two small groups that result, explain your choice and discuss your attitudes about and experiences with reading the Bible. Then share your findings with the whole group. Did the discussion generate any insights or practical suggestions that might enhance your encounters with God through the Bible?

enriching. As with prayer, it may help to try several different methods of studying the Bible. Once they get started, many people

---

Biblical Studies 101: *Jesus' Need for Solitude*

Although we commonly envision Jesus in ministry with other people, Jesus' life was a model of balance between community and solitude. Many passages in the Bible describe times when Jesus left the company of others to be alone with God. Read Matthew 4:1-11; 14:13-23; Mark 1:35-39; 14:32-42; Luke 5:15-16; and 6:12-16. In preparation for his ministry, Jesus, led by the Holy Spirit, spent 40 days alone in the desert. He spent the night praying alone on a mountainside before choosing his twelve apostles from among his followers. After the miracle of feeding 5,000 people, he sent his disciples ahead of him and spent some time in solitary prayer. Although his ministry of preaching, teaching, and healing kept him in constant contact with people, he frequently withdrew from the crowds to find quiet places to pray. And to ready himself for his betrayal and crucifixion, Jesus left his disciples to keep vigil while he prayed alone in the garden of Gethsemane. Throughout his ministry, Jesus recognized the necessity of time alone with God in order to receive the guidance and strength he needed to carry out God's will.

Jesus' Need for Solitude
Read the six Scripture passages again that are listed in the Biblical Studies 101 box. Why do you think solitude was so important to Jesus? What do you think Jesus' life and ministry would have been like if he had not taken time for solitude? Do you think it is possible to have a close relationship with God without solitude? How much of your time do you spend in solitude? How much of your solitary time do you devote to God? If you spent more time alone with God, how do you think your life would change?

find Bible study an indispensable part of their daily routine. According to Delia Halverson in *Living Simply* (Abingdon Press, 1996), it takes six weeks to establish a habit, so be patient and keep going.

CELEBRATING TOGETHER

While time alone with God is essential, we were not meant to practice our faith in isolation. Read Psalm 95:1-7; Matthew 7:7-8; and Hebrews 10:23-25. These passages call us to worship, pray, and have fellowship together.

Corporate worship can be a very effective way to encounter God. Look back to the story of Pentecost we read earlier in Acts 2. When the community of believers came together, the Holy Spirit came upon them and empowered them to engage in Christ's ministry. We, too, can experience the joy of

God's presence and gain new energy for service when we join together to worship God.

An enormous variety of worship experiences are available today. It seems that God has created churches as wonderfully diverse as God created us. If worship is not a part of your life, find a church that feeds your soul. You owe it to God—and yourself.

SERVICE: GOD IS OUT THERE

Read John 13:1-20. It was the night of Jesus' betrayal, and he was sharing a meal with his disciples for one last time. To everyone's astonishment, Jesus started the evening by performing the unpleasant task of a hired servant: washing his disciples' dusty feet. In this profound act, Jesus' point was clear: As followers of Christ, we must humble ourselves and serve one another.

Although serving others may not immediately come to mind when we think about spiritual disciplines, humble service can be one of the most exhilarating ways to experi-

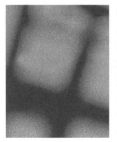

ence God's presence. According to Howard Clinebell, "Caring outreach is one of the most important things you can do to increase your own well being." If your spiritual life feels stagnant, perhaps some tangible acts of loving service can help revitalize your relationship with God.

OVERCOMING BARRIERS

The most common barriers to a devotional life are simply finding time and space

Celebrating Together

Is it possible to be a Christian in isolation? Why is a community of faith important? What, if any, spiritual nourishment can you derive from a group experience that you can't get with just you and God? Have you ever taken part of a group experience where you have been acutely aware of God's presence? If so, describe the experience.

How often do you worship God? To what extent does your own attitude toward worship influence the degree of fulfillment you gain from it? If the primary purpose of worship is to honor God, how much does your own satisfaction really matter?

Service: God Is Out There

Why do you think service was the key to Jenna's (page 43) relationship with God? Using your own life as a case study, recall a time when you felt uplifted by an act of service. (Read John 13:1-20.) Why do you think your action had such a positive effect on you? What does this example of Jesus' service show you? Or, recall a time when God seemed remote. Do you think some caring outreach on your part could have brought you closer to God? Why or why not? What types of service is God calling you to now?

Overcoming Barriers

How can you make time in your busy schedule for a devotional life? What prevents you from doing so? What do you think is the more difficult barrier: lack of time, or the way you prioritize your time? What, if anything, would you be willing to give up in order to have a closer relationship with God? What other barriers get in the way of a richer devotional life for you? How might you overcome them?

List some devotional activities that you would like to do if time were not a limitation. Brainstorm ways you might incorporate these activities into your schedule.

Your Challenge

Take a few minutes of silence to envision the relationship with God described by Richard Foster. Then pray about your own relationship with God. Do any aspects of your devotional life need more attention? What, if anything, is God calling you to do to enrich your spiritual life? If you are comfortable doing so, share your insights and your pledge for the week with the rest of the group.

Close with a group prayer, asking God to make God's presence felt in the life of each person and the group as a whole. Pray that God will guide you in your devotional life and make your efforts fruitful.

in our busy schedules. There is no simple answer to these problems, but the effort to find solutions will be well worth it. Remember Dan from the "Getting Started" section? As busy as he was, his life ran much more smoothly when he took time daily to spend with God.

Applying our concept of "both/and solutions" to the time and space problem may help. Think back to our question from Session 2: What is short-changed in your life? If it is solitude, wake up a half-hour earlier than everyone else in your household and use the time for prayer and study. If it is exercise, take a prayer walk during your lunch hour, or read the Bible while on the treadmill. If it is time with others away from the pressures of work, join a Christian group with an active fellowship or service program. One busy parent found that the morning shower was the only opportunity for solitude all day, and thus the best time to be open to God's voice. Be creative and use the resources available to you.

YOUR CHALLENGE

In the *Wrestling With Angels* video series (Zondervan Video, 1993), Richard Foster describes his experience with God as "an ongoing, developing love relationship." As he grew in this relationship, Foster experienced "the utter availability of God and the utter accessibility of God."

Does this describe your relationship with God? If not, what is lacking in your spiritual life? Challenge yourself this week to make God your top priority for at least a part of each day. Use this daily time of "putting God first" to engage in some spiritual practice that will bring you closer to God and help open yourself up to God's transforming power.

IT TAKES TWO (OR MORE)

This session will explore issues of balance in our closest personal relationships of family and friends.

GETTING STARTED

Dixon: I really love my family, but I have a hard time expressing it. And, to be honest, sometimes I guess I act just the opposite. My temper gets the best of me, and I say things I don't mean. I know my words hurt, and I wish I could take them back, but once they're out of my mouth it's too late.

Joy: I've been in several bad relationships where I've been exploited and manipulated. But all I hear from the church is how I'm supposed to submit to authority and forgive. It sounds like God wants me to put up with the abuse. Am I really supposed to be a doormat?

Caroline: The Bible is full of God's call to sacrificial love. I want to obey God, but I don't think I'll ever be ready to give everything up for someone else. How can I love like God wants me to without losing myself in the process?

Greet one another and welcome newcomers. Briefly share your experiences of carrying out your pledge (from Session 4) to focus on your spiritual life. What happened when you made God your top priority for a part of every day? How did you use this time? Did it change you or your relationship with God? If so, how?

Can you identify with any of the people in the "Getting Started" section? If so, how? What might the people do to find greater balance? Share some of your own experiences and any insights you have gained about how to attain greater balance in your close relationships.

All You Need Is Love
Read John 13:33-35 again. Keeping in mind Jesus' commandment to love one another, make a word web on love. (See page 20.) What insights did you gain about the biblical concept of loving relationships?

Think of a time when you felt especially close to the people with whom you share your life. Share your stories in pairs. What made this time so special? Do you think it is possible to experience this degree of closeness all the time? Why or why not? How could you and your loved ones experience this degree of closeness more often? What barriers prevent you from doing so?

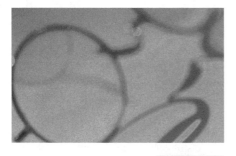

It's Not That Easy
Re-read Gail O'Day's quote on loving one another. Do you agree with her statement? Why or why not? Do you ever find it difficult to love those closest to you? If so, why? In what ways do we treat strangers, casual acquaintances, or even people we know but do not especially like, better than the ones we love?

Dale: I've been hurt in relationships before and that makes me hesitant to get close to people. I know God wants us to forgive, but it's really hard. How can I let go and get on with my life?

ALL YOU NEED IS LOVE

Read John 13:33-35. Jesus addressed these words to his disciples during the Last Supper, shortly after washing their feet to illustrate his vision of loving service. In the same manner that he explained his act of foot-washing in John 13:14, Jesus told his disciples, "Just as I have loved you, you also should love one another." Jesus loved his friends so much that he was about to die on the cross for them. Jesus exhorted his disciples to demonstrate an equally sacrificial love for the people closest to them, those within their own faith community.

In the previous chapter, we explored how a vital relationship with God provides an indispensable foundation to a balanced life. However, as the above Scripture passage illustrates, maintaining this relationship in a vacuum is not what God intended. God calls us to live out our faith in our relationships with others, starting with those closest to us.

IT'S NOT THAT EASY

According to the old expression, charity begins at home. Ideally, we ought to be able to say the same about love. But while Jesus' commandment to love one another may sound simple, anyone who has experienced the convolutions of close relationships among family and friends knows that reality can be far more complicated. Gail O'Day, a New Testament scholar, wrote, "It is no easy task for

Christians to love one another. In many ways, it is easier to love one's enemies, because one might not have to deal with them every day."

Read 1 Corinthians 13:4-7. We usually associate these words with the joyous occasion of a wedding ceremony, but Paul intended these words for a whole community of believers. This passage is part of Paul's response to serious problems within the fledgling Christian church in Corinth, Greece. Instead of loving one another, the Corinthians engaged in hostile arguments, divided themselves into factions, and sued each other in court. By abusing their relationships in these ways, the Corinthian Christians were hurting each other and setting a very negative example for those outside the faith. Paul wrote to remind them that love is at the very core of being a follower of Christ.

What does it really mean to "love one another"? And why is loving our loved ones so hard sometimes? There are no easy answers to these questions, and Christians have been struggling with them since their earliest days. Even Jesus' close relationships were difficult at times.

Read 1 Corinthians 13:4-7 again, keeping in mind that Paul wrote it to a congregation in conflict. Have you ever witnessed unloving behavior or unbalanced relationships within a church congregation or other faith-based group? Explain. If love is so central to our faith, why is there such conflict and strife within faith communities? What can we do about it?

Jesus' Relationships
Read the six Scripture passages again. Do you think his relationships with his loved ones were balanced? Why? How did Jesus balance his responsibilities to God with his obligations to family and close friends? Do you think his loved ones always understood his actions? What can this story teach us about our own relationships?

Biblical Studies 101: *Jesus' Close Relationships*

It is clear from Scripture that Jesus engaged in close relationships throughout his life. Although the Bible never discusses Jesus' marital status, we know that he had close family relationships as a son and brother and intimate friendships with his disciples and others. Among his close friends were women, a radical departure from social convention in first-century Palestine. As the following Scripture passages illustrate, Jesus' relationships were sometimes complicated. Jesus performed his first public miracle at Cana to obey his mother, despite his own objections (John 2:1-12). Later, Jesus did not even acknowledge his family when they tried to restrain him from preaching to a hostile crowd (Mark 3:19b-35). For two days, Jesus ignored his close friends' plea to help their dying brother (John 11:1-44). And Jesus' most intimate relationships with his disciples were sometimes marred by their jealousy (Mark 10:35-45). However, Scripture leaves no doubt that Jesus loved his friends (John 15:12-17) and family (John 19:25b-27). Even in the midst of some very human problems, Jesus' relationships serve as a model of love, loyalty, and compassionate concern.

Taming the Tongue

Take a few moments to reflect silently on a time when you lost control of your tongue. Why did you say what you did? How did your words affect the people you love? How did you feel when you saw the consequences of your words? Did your speech or behavior change after the incident? Take some time to express your feelings about the incident creatively, perhaps by writing a poem or sketching a picture. If you are comfortable doing so, share your story and your expression of it with others in your group.

DISCUSS

Read James 3:1-12 again. What are the consequences of an untamed tongue? Does James offer any advice on how we might control our speech? Have you ever tried to tame your tongue? If so, how? How successful were your efforts? As a group, take several minutes to brainstorm some practical strategies for keeping hurtful speech in check.

TAMING THE TONGUE

One of the most obvious ways we can love our loved ones is to speak to them with loving respect. The words that come out of our mouths have enormous power to build up or tear down the people we love. Proverbs 15:1 and 4 aptly describe the power of words: "A soft answer turns away wrath, / but a harsh word stirs up anger." A gentle tongue is a tree of life, / but perverseness in it breaks the spirit."

Read James 3:1-12. This passage, part of a letter instructing early Christians in moral behavior, emphasizes the destructive power of speech. The author asserts that it is impossible for humans to control the tongue, which he describes as "a restless evil, full of deadly poison." James points out the contradiction of using our tongue to bless God and curse people. When we use our words to hurt others who are made in the image of God, we are, in effect, hurting God.

Remember Dixon from the "Getting Started" section? His inability to control his words caused harm to his family and guilt in himself. Unfortunately, Dixon's scenario is not unique. In her book, *The Verbally Abusive Relationship* (Adams Media Corporation, 1996), Patricia Evans wrote "Verbal abuse is, in a sense, built into our culture. One-upmanship, defeating, putting down, topping, countering, manipulating, criticizing, hard selling, and intimidating are accepted as fair games by many. When these power plays are enacted in a relationship confusion results." Words, when used destructively, are deadly weapons that can throw loving relationships out of balance.

DOES GOD WANT ME TO BE A DOORMAT?

God calls us to gentle speech and action in all our relationships. In Philippians 4:5, Paul encourages Christians to "let your gentleness be known to everyone." In 1 Peter 3:16, Christians were told that even when confronted with intimidation by non-believers, they should defend their faith "with gentleness and reverence." Sometimes, however, the line between practicing godly gentleness and allowing ourselves to be treated unfairly is very fine. In an unbalanced intimate relationship, the line may seem blurred beyond recognition. Earlier, we read that love "bears all things" (1 Corinthians 13:7). As Christians, just how much are we supposed to put up with?

Read Ephesians 5:21. In this letter to the early Ephesian church, Paul instructed the congregation on the importance of deferring to others in their Christian relationships. Although the verses that follow (which call for submission of wives to husbands, children to parents, and slaves to masters) are well known, many people fail to place them in the proper context of the overarching command of verse 21 to submit to one another in all our Christian relationships. The mutual submission Paul calls for is ultimately rooted in our submission to God. In this context, mutual submission is a vital and healthy component of a loving relationship.

Unfortunately, human love, unlike God's love, is not perfect. How are we to respond when submission is not mutual? Joy's question from the "Getting Started" section echoes the uncertainty many of us feel when trying to live godly lives in the context of hurtful relationships.

Does God Want Me to Be a Doormat?
Read Ephesians 5:21–6:9. Using at least two different Bible commentaries, read background material and others' interpretations of this passage. How do you interpret the passage? What, if any, relevance does it have in our society today? If God calls us to mutual submission, why are the other submission passages in Ephesians 5 and 6 necessary? How are we to reconcile them with what we know about God's universal love and justice?

Read Joy's statement from the opening dialogue. As a Christian, how do you think she should respond in relationships where she is exploited or manipulated? At what point does an unbalanced relationship become an abusive one? What is the church's responsibility to people like Joy? to her partner? If you are comfortable doing so, share examples of how you have struggled with similar questions in your own life. (Note that this can be a very painful subject and no one should feel obligated to share. Treat what you hear carefully and confidentially.) How are we to apply biblical teachings about forgiveness and submission in unbalanced or abusive relationships? Where can we turn if the ones we love hurt us? How can we support others when it happens to them?

Read Matthew 18:15-17 again. How practical are these instructions today for resolving conflict within a faith community? Can you think of any examples where this process has been used? How is this process relevant to conflict resolution in a non-church setting? Would it be appropriate to use this process to help resolve conflict in a couple or a family? Why or why not? How do you interpret Jesus' instructions in Matthew 18:17? (In developing your response, consider how Jesus regarded Gentiles and tax collectors.)

Letting Go: Restoring the Balance

Read Matthew 18:21-22.
Why do you think Jesus said these words to Peter? How do you interpret this passage? Where do you draw the line on forgiveness? Why? Who benefits when you forgive? Does Jesus' instruction call you to change anything about the way you forgive others?

Read Matthew 18:15-17. Jesus' instructions about how to respond when sinned against by someone in church reflect the reality that at some point we are likely to be hurt by someone close to us. Jesus' advice was to try to work out the problem in three stages as needed: first, one-on-one; then with one or two other people to serve as witnesses; and, if necessary, publicly in front of the whole fellowship. The passage implies that if the offender refuses to change his or her behavior even when confronted by the whole church, the wronged party has done everything possible and is no longer bound to continue the relationship. Jesus' process helps to ensure that even if a relationship ends, all parties are treated with dignity while trying to settle the matter.

Jesus came so we could have full and abundant lives (John 10:10b). While mutual submission is godly, God clearly does not want us to be abused. Unfortunately, being a Christian is no guarantee that we will never be hurt in a relationship. The good news is that even if our loved ones let us down, nothing can separate us from the love of God (Romans 8:38-39).

LETTING GO: RESTORING THE BALANCE

Eventually, if trust is violated in a relationship, we must pick ourselves up and move on. This is true whether the relationship continues or ends. Although easier said than done, we will never be able to regain balance in our lives if we are unable to put past hurts behind us.

An essential component in this process, and one of the most basic concepts in the Christian faith, is forgiveness. Every time we pray the Lord's Prayer we are reminded that Jesus taught us to forgive those who have sinned against us. In Matthew 18:21-22, Jesus instructed Peter to forgive not seven but seventy-seven times. But where do we draw the line between godly forgiveness and unhealthy enabling? And how can we forgive when someone we love has caused such pain?

Read John 8:1-11. In his encounter with the angry throng about to stone a woman, Jesus' words led the crowd to realize that none of them was without sin. Consequently, none of them could bring themselves to condemn her. The woman left, free and forgiven, with the charge of taking responsibility for her future actions. In the same way, reflecting on our own roles in failed relationships may help us to forgive those who mistreat us, without condoning their sin or minimizing its impact, and move on.

Forgiveness, although essential, is only part of the answer. In order to move on with our lives we also must let go of the past. The first step is realizing that there is absolutely nothing we can do to change our past. Acknowledging that we have no control over the past frees us to focus our energies on our present and future. Paraphrasing the words of the Serenity Prayer, we need to accept the things we cannot change, change the things we can, and learn to discern between the two.

SELF AND OTHERS: SETTING PRIORITIES

In the "Getting Started" section, Caroline wondered if it were possible to love someone without losing herself in the process. Fortunately, God does not force us to make

Read John 8:1-11 again three times, putting yourself in the place of a different character from the story: the accusing crowd, the accused woman, and Jesus. Imagine what you would think and feel in each case. Then think of corresponding situations from your own experience when you (1) accused someone and were unwilling to forgive; (2) needed forgiveness; and (3) exercised your power to forgive. How did you feel in each real-life situation? How might you approach similar situations in the future?

Sing or say the hymn "This Is a Day of New Beginnings." What does this hymn tell us about letting go? How can faith in God help us to move on from past hurts and mistakes in our relationships? Tell about a time you experienced a "new beginning" in a close relationship.

Self and Others
How much of your time do you devote to your loved ones? to yourself? How does that allocation correspond to your priorities in life? What do you do for self-care? What individual interests do you nurture? Do your individual pursuits enhance your close relationships in any way? How can we set aside time for self-care without sacrificing time with our loved ones? Brainstorm practical suggestions and "both/and" solutions.

It Takes Two (Or More)

an either/or choice between loving others and ourselves. Jesus' words in Mark 12:31 demonstrate that God expects us to love and care for ourselves as well as others. If we deny ourselves to the point of losing our God-given individuality, we will have very little left to offer back to God or to the people we love. God's vision of Christian relationships is therefore a both/and proposition: To love others, we must learn to love ourselves.

How can we balance our own needs with those of our partners in relationships? Perhaps the answer lies in setting priorities and allocating our time and energy accordingly. We know that time together is essential for any relationship to succeed. However, it is also important to make self-care a priority. This means carving out time for ourselves in the midst of our busy schedules. If all parties in a relationship can agree to some time apart to nurture their own interests, sharing their experiences during time spent together can further strengthen their bond.

SMALL GROUP

Your Challenge
Spend some time in silence to think of someone with whom you have a difficult relationship. Pray about this relationship over the coming week, asking God for guidance in restoring the balance. Then perform some tangible act of love toward that person. Afterward, reflect on your action. How did your action affect the other person? How did it affect you? Did it change your relationship in any way? If you wish, share your thoughts from your silent reflection with the rest of the group. How do you feel about this week's challenge?

YOUR CHALLENGE

In the award-winning movie *The Apostle*, the main character was a pastor whose closest relationships became so unbalanced that he alienated his family, lost his job, and nearly destroyed himself.

Are your personal relationships in balance? If not, what is out of kilter? What do others need from you that you are not giving? What do you need that you are not getting? And where does God fit into the picture? Pledge to change one thing about how you interact with your loved ones this week that will bring you closer together and make your relationships more balanced.

CLOSE

Close with group prayer, asking God for strength and guidance as we strive for greater balance in our difficult relationships. Everyone should feel free to pray aloud or pass. Close by asking for God's intervention in all our close relationships.

IT'S NOT FAIR!

> This session will explore the concept of biblical justice and how it relates to a balanced Christian lifestyle.

GETTING STARTED

Derek: I run a tutoring center for disadvantaged kids. We're about to lose our funding grant because our enrollment increased and our teacher-student ratio is under the minimum requirement. We can't afford another teacher. If we turn away kids, they'll end up on the street. The only way to keep our funding and stay open is to lie about the numbers. I know lying is wrong, but I'm really tempted to do it anyway.

Maria: "WWJD—What Would Jesus Do?" I hear this all the time from some of my Christian friends, and it makes things sound so clear-cut. But how do they know what Jesus would do? Do they have a monopoly on the truth? I wish I could be as sure as they are.

Jerome: Christians are supposed to stand up for justice, right? But some of the most unjust behavior I've ever seen has happened right here in church. Is the church immune to God's teaching on justice? Why is it so hard for Christians to practice what they preach?

Getting Started

Greet one another and welcome newcomers. Briefly share your experiences of carrying out your pledge (from Session 5) to perform a tangible act of love toward someone with whom you have a difficult relationship. What did you do, and why did you choose to do it? How did your action make you feel? How did it affect the person for whom you did it?

Can you identify with any of the people in the "Getting Started" section? If so, how? What is the justice issue in each of their statements? How do you think these issues relate to balance? Share some of your own experiences dealing with similar situations. What justice issues have you faced, and how did you decide what to do about them? What role did your faith play in your decisions?

Sophie: I see injustice going on at work. I know people who were denied promotions or restricted from key meetings just because of their race or sexual orientation. It makes me sick—but I don't know what to do about it. I need my job, and I'm afraid of the consequences if I speak out. Where do I draw the line between standing up for justice and self-preservation?

BIBLICAL JUSTICE

Read Amos 5:21-24 and Micah 6:6-8. These powerful words of the Old Testament prophets tell us in no uncertain terms that our God is a God of justice. Written eight centuries before Christ in the midst of a society characterized by wide chasms between the rich and mighty and the poor and oppressed, the prophets' words warned of dire consequences if people ignored God's call to righteous behavior. Speaking on God's behalf, the prophets cautioned that religious ritual and showy offerings were meaningless if unaccompanied by just behavior.

The ancient writings of Amos and Micah are still relevant today. Imbalance exists within our own communities in the form of wide gulfs between the privileged and the disadvantaged. People continue to be denied opportunities based on characteristics of their birth or background. And as Christians living in a society where oppression occurs, we participate in it either through our action or passivity. If the prophets were writing today, perhaps they would warn that our own religious practice may displease God if the words we use in worship do not correspond to our everyday actions. What God really wants from God's people is justice and righteousness.

SMALL GROUP

Biblical Justice
Form two groups, one to work with the concept of "rights" and the other, "righteousness." In your group, take 3 minutes to brainstorm (and write down) all the words or phrases that come to mind when you think of your concept. Then share your results with the other group. How do the two lists compare? Can you think of any situations where the pursuit of rights might be unrighteous? Can the pursuit of righteousness ever violate someone's rights? Explain. In situations where rights and righteousness conflict, how do you respond?

In a balanced community, all persons are treated as the images of God they are. The idea of balance is therefore inseparable from the biblical concept of justice. But what, exactly, is justice? Many people equate justice with individual rights, and certainly our society leaves room for improvement in this regard. However, justice in the biblical sense focuses on righteousness, which encompasses far more than personal rights.

According to David Gill, author of *Becoming Good* (InterVarsity Press, 2000), "A Biblical righteousness/justice is not first of all human centered but God-centered. It is not narrowly or statically rights-oriented but is dynamic and embraces the whole of God's character and the whole of our life. God's call to be righteous and just is a call to conform to [God's] standard of righteous thought and action. It means to hunger to know, understand and apply what God is, says, and does."

THE RIGHT THING

Fulfilling Gill's vision of biblical justice is a rather tall order, for it calls us to apply God's standard of justice in all of our personal decisions. And to do so, we must have some sense of how God would want us to act. Sometimes, the just course of action is obvious. But other situations are more complicated, and the "right thing" may not be clear. Derek's dilemma is a good example. At times like this, how are we to know the will of God?

And even if we understand what righteous behavior is, how can we be inspired to live righteously? According to a 1999 poll by *U.S. News*, 1 in 4 adults believe they have to lie and cheat to get ahead. In a cul-

Read Amos 5:21-24 and Micah 6:6-8 again. Think about what these passages mean, and rewrite them in your own words in the context of contemporary life. Share your results with the rest of the group. As Christians, are there any ways in which our behavior contradicts what we say or do in worship, or what we profess to believe? If so, how and why? What would we need to do to bring our faith and actions closer together?

The Right Thing
Look back to Derek's statement in the "Getting Started" section. If you were Derek, how would you respond, and why? How does your faith influence your response? Can you think of any other options that Derek didn't consider? If you have faced a similar situation, share it with the rest of the group. How did you respond, and why? Do you think your response met God's standard of justice? Why or why not?

Why do you think 25 percent of American adults surveyed believe they must lie or cheat to get ahead? Does this statistic shock you, or does it conform to your experience? Can you think of any famous people who are glorified for their ability to cheat? Are lying and cheating always unethical? Do righteous ends ever justify unethical means? Have you ever been tempted to lie or cheat for personal gain? for a good cause? If so, share how you felt during the experience. What do you do when you are tempted to cheat? What do you do when you see others cheat?

The Bible Tells Me So—
Read 2 Timothy 3:14-16 and 2 Peter 3:14-18 again. What does each of these passages say about the authority of Scripture? What do you believe about the authority of Scripture? Do you give some parts of the Bible more weight than others? If so, which ones, and why?

Have you ever been faced with a difficult decision and found guidance in the Bible? If so, share your story. How did Scripture help you decide what to do? Where else do you turn for answers when you struggle to discern what is right?

ture where cutting ethical corners is so common, where can we find the strength to live out God's will?

Fortunately, through Jesus, God came to live among us. Jesus' life serves as our ultimate model of, and inspiration for, the righteous behavior God expects of us. By studying Jesus' and the early church's responses to common human situations, we can learn a great deal about justice. And the Bible is our single best source of information for doing so.

THE BIBLE TELLS ME SO—

Read 2 Timothy 3:14-16 and 2 Peter 3:14-18. The second letter of Paul to Timothy calls all Scripture "God-breathed" and useful for training Christians in righteous behavior. The second letter of Peter to Christians scattered throughout Asia Minor affirms the importance of Scripture, including Paul's letters, but also warns readers of the dangers of twisting and misinterpreting them.

How much authority should we give to the words of the Bible? Are certain parts more important than others? What should we do when different passages appear to contradict each other? And how do we discern what is right in situations that are not treated in the Bible? As helpful as Scripture is in teaching us about righteous behavior, sometimes its guidance seems unclear. This ambiguity can be frustrating, as reflected by Maria's words in the opening dialogue.

How do we discern the righteous path when Scripture offers no obvious answers? One way is to pray about the matter, asking for God's guidance. Another is to apply our God-given gifts of intellect and conscience to the situation. John Wesley, an eighteenth-century evangelist and the founder of Methodism, proposed using Scripture, Christian tradition, personal experience, and our ability to reason as tools in our process of spiritual discernment, and many Christians continue to find these guidelines helpful today.

JUSTICE IN THE CHURCH

Read Matthew 18:10-14. In this parable, Jesus tells of a shepherd who left his flock of a hundred sheep to search for one that was lost. We usually think of the lost sheep as having left the flock of its own accord. However, in a pastoral letter from May 2000, United Methodist Bishop C. Joseph Sprague proposed another scenario: "I have come to perceive that the one sheep outside the fold just might have been driven out by the 99 others." Do we, intentionally or unintentionally, exclude anyone from our communities of faith? Read Romans 15:1-7; Galatians 3:23-29; and Ephesians 4:1-6. In all of these letters to churches under his guidance, Paul's theme is clear: Through Christ, all believers are accepted equally by God and any divisions among the faithful must fall away. Paul exhorted church members to "live in harmony with one another" and "welcome one another just as Christ has welcomed you" (Romans 15:5, 7). Differences in ethnic background, gender and social status became meaningless once people embraced faith in Jesus Christ.

This unity represents God's vision of justice as it is to be practiced in the church. And many churches strive to fulfill this vision of acceptance of and equal respect for all believers. As with any human insti-

BIBLE

Justice in the Church
Read Matthew 18:10-14 again. What do you think about Bishop Sprague's interpretation of this passage? Who is not represented in your church or other Christian groups? Is their lack of presence due to intentional exclusion or other factors? If other factors, what are they? What could you and your faith community do to overcome these barriers? What prevents you from doing so?

Read Romans 15:1-7; Galatians 3:23-29; and Ephesians 4:1-6. How are these passages relevant to justice issues within your own congregations? Based on your understanding of these Scriptures and your own experience, how would you respond to Jerome's criticism in the "Getting Started" section?

SMALL GROUP

Think of a time when you felt like an outsider in church or another setting. What happened to make you feel that way? How did you react? Express your feelings about this time artistically by drawing a sketch or writing a poem. In pairs, share your story and artistry. What could others in this setting have done to make you feel like you belonged? What can you learn from your experience about how to make others feel welcome in your faith community? Share your responses to the last question with the whole group.

tution, however, churches may fall short of God's standard. Many Christian churches are struggling with issues of inclusion and equality regarding race, gender, marital status, sexual orientation, socioeconomic class, and disabilities. When, as Christians, we fail to welcome one another as Christ welcomed us, we invite the criticism voiced by Jerome in the opening dialogue.

RETRIBUTION OR MERCY?

Read Matthew 5:38-42 and Romans 12:17-21. These passages illustrate Jesus' radical new framework for the biblical concept of justice. God's law of "an eye for an eye and a tooth for a tooth" (Exodus 21:24), allowed for some violence but prevented unlimited revenge by insisting that punishment fit the crime. In contrast, Jesus taught his followers to "turn the other cheek." Paul exhorted Christians to "never avenge yourselves," but instead, to "overcome evil with good."

These New Testament teachings appear to leave no room for retribution or revenge from anyone's hand but God's. Instead, Jesus calls for a merciful response. In essence, this means relinquishing the right to hurt someone back, or even to hold a grudge.

In a society where even trivial disagreements often end up in court, how do we apply these teachings? Does the biblical prohibition on retribution mean we should not pursue any legal redress for injustices suffered? Shouldn't those committing injustice be punished, or at least deterred from continuing to do so? Although answers to these questions may not be obvious, one thing is clear: Restraining ourselves from retribution does not mean we should sit back and watch while injustice occurs.

STAND UP FOR JUSTICE

Read 2 Samuel 11:1-12:14. The biblical saga of David and Bathsheba reads like a soap opera. David enjoyed great power as a result of God's favor. Unfortunately, he abused this power and sinned against God by committing adultery with Bathsheba and ordering the murder of her husband Uriah. God sent the prophet Nathan to confront David about the gravity of his injustice. As king, it was in David's power to imprison or kill Nathan for his unpleasant message, but that did not stop Nathan from speaking out.

Fortunately for Nathan, David accepted God's condemnation and repented without harming the messenger. But other justice advocates in Christian history have met with harsh punishment or even death for taking a stand. Acts 6:8-8:1 tells of Stephen, who was stoned to death for standing up for his Christian beliefs. More recently, one of the saddest chapters in American history is the assassination of Martin Luther King, Jr. for his prophetic stand against racial injustice.

The Other Cheek

Think of a time when you were treated unjustly. How did you feel? Did your response most closely resemble passive acceptance, violent retribution, or nonviolent action? Did your response make you feel better or worse? Reread Matthew 5:38-39. If you faced the same situation again, how would you react, in light of this Scripture?

Stand for Justice

Read 2 Samuel 11:1-12:15 aloud, with group members reading or acting out the parts of the various characters, then discuss Nathan and David's conversation. How do you think Nathan felt when God sent him to see David? How did Nathan's method of confronting David help David acknowledge his sin and repent? What would you have done in Nathan's situation? What can we learn from this story about how to react when we witness injustice?

Biblical Studies 101: *Turning the Other Cheek*

Read Matthew 5:38-39. Jesus' instruction to his disciples to "turn the other cheek" if struck in the face is often interpreted as an unequivocal call for passive submission. However, theologian Walter Wink asserts that Jesus' command was really a call to active nonviolent resistance. As Wink explains it, the specification of a strike on the right cheek indicates a back-handed blow intended to demean more than injure. By turning the other (left) cheek to accept another right-handed blow instead of submitting passively, the victim would face the oppressor as a human being of equal statusr. This symbolic gesture would, in effect, affirm the dignity of the victim while robbing the oppressor of the ability to humiliate. With this teaching, Jesus renounced both passive submission and violent retribution as responses to injustice, advocating nonviolent action instead.

Read Sophie's statement in the "Getting Started" section. What would you have done in her situation? Have you ever witnessed injustice but feared the consequences of taking action? When faced with such a dilemma, how do we balance our own security with the greater good? In what ways can standing up for justice harm us or others? Can seeing injustice and not taking action ever be a faithful response? Why or why not?

Your Challenge

CLOSE

Spend some time in silence to think about injustice you see around you. Then take a blank piece of paper and divide it into two columns. In the left column, write down any specific ways in which you might be contributing to unjust situations, either through your action or inaction. Pray about this list over the coming week, asking God to show you specific actions you can take to stand up for justice. Write these "just responses" in the right column on your paper. Pledge to perform at least one tangible act this week to fight injustice. If you are comfortable doing so, share the results of your silent reflection with the rest of the group. What unjust situations do you have the power to influence? To which do you feel most drawn to respond? Close with group prayer, asking God for guidance and strength to stand up for justice.

As people of faith, how can we stand up for justice? And what are the consequences of doing so? Look back to Sophie in the "Getting Started" section. She saw injustice in her company, but felt powerless to act without making herself vulnerable. In situations like Sophie's, how do we balance our need for security with our call to stand up for the common good?

For Christians, justice is not an abstract concept that we can leave in the hands of lawyers, judges, and civil rights advocates. Justice is something we must practice as a lifestyle. Everything we do, from our smallest ethical decisions to our interactions with our families, co-workers, fellow Christians, and all others should be grounded in the vision of justice provided by Jesus. When we confront justice issues in our daily lives, every action we choose to take or not take has a consequence. If the right course of action is not clear, we must ask for God's guidance and the courage to follow it.

YOUR CHALLENGE

In his 1963 letter from the Birmingham city jail, Martin Luther King, Jr. wrote, "Injustice anywhere is a threat to justice everywhere." Take some time to examine your life honestly. Are you participating in any form of injustice toward others? Are you observing any injustice going on, but not doing anything about it? If so, it is time

to have a heart-to-heart talk with God. Challenge yourself this week to seek earnestly God's direction in confronting your own role in unjust situations and taking the appropriate action to respond.

JUSTICE GOES GLOBAL

> This session will explore how God's justice calls us to strive for balance and shalom among all of God's creation.

GETTING STARTED

Cara: When we look at balance on a global scale, everything seems so complex. There's such great need, but the needs compete with each other. If we build roads for economic development, the environment suffers. If we boycott companies because of low wages in their overseas factories, destitute families could be deprived of their only source of income. If we take any action at all, we risk making things worse! So much is political. How can we sort it all out?

Cliff: Whenever I hear about global justice, it's usually associated with some appeal for money. I consider myself one of the "have-nots" of the world. I only recently managed to get myself off the streets, and I don't have an extra penny to spare. I care about problems in the rest of the world, but what can I do about them? Isn't that the responsibility of the rich?

Iliana: Blaming the problems on politics is a cop-out. It's just a conve-

START — Greet one another and welcome newcomers. Briefly share your experiences of carrying out your pledge (from Session 6) to perform at least one tangible act to fight injustice. What did you do and why? What was the effect on you and on others? Do you feel God is leading you to further action? If so, how will you proceed?

CASE STUDY — Can you identify with any of the people in the "Getting Started" section? If so, how? Share your own experiences with global justice issues or questions you may have about them. How has your faith influenced the way you look at those issues?

nient way for us to shirk our own responsibility. We'll never make a difference unless we change our own lifestyles in radical ways. And we have to speak out so others will change, too. I think that's what God calls us to do.

Russ: I don't want to be a radical, and I don't think God wants that either. We're called to be peaceful, and that just doesn't fit with being an extremist. Christians aren't supposed to make trouble.

WHO IS MY NEIGHBOR?

Read Luke 10:25-37. Jesus told this parable to a lawyer who, in reference to God's command to "love your neighbor as yourself," asked Jesus, "And who is my neighbor?" When we read this story, we usually frame it in terms of the lawyer's question, trying to discern who should be the object of our compassion and good works. If we read the parable closely, however, we see that Jesus turned this question on its head by asking, "Which of these three, do you think, was a neighbor to the man who fell into the hands of the robbers?" Instead of focusing on the person *in need of* justice, he identified the neighbor as the one *doing* justice.

In Jesus' parable, the priest and the Levite, two religious authorities, intentionally avoided the injured man, but the Samaritan went out of his way to approach him. Jesus must have shocked his audience by portraying the neighbor as a Samaritan, an ethnic group reviled by the Jews and treated as outcasts.

What are the implications of this parable for us? First, Jesus calls us to be neighbors. Second, instead of waiting for others to approach us and ask for justice, we must be willing to leave the comfort of our own routines and actively seek out those in need. Third, as neighbors we are called to cross the social, cultural, and economic boundaries that might otherwise divide us. Fourth, we all have a responsibility to act justly, even if we are at the bottom rung of the socio-economic ladder or, like the Samaritan, are ourselves victims of injustice. Following these biblical guidelines would go a long way toward bringing more balance to God's world.

WHAT'S WRONG WITH THIS PICTURE?

Read 2 Corinthians 8:8-15. Paul used these words to encourage the members of the Corinthian church to share their resources generously with Christian congregations elsewhere. Paul did not ask the Corinthians to impoverish themselves to make others rich, but to give within their means to help others whose means were lacking. Paul viewed such sharing as a simple matter of fairness: There should be "fair balance" between the abundance of some and the needs of others.

Unfortunately, Paul's vision of fair balance is far from reality today. According to Bread for the World, a Christian justice organization, over half the people in the world survive on less than two dollars a day. The wealthiest fifth of the world's population consumes 86 percent of the world's resources, while the poorest fifth consumes only about 1 percent. Even in the United States 10 percent of households face the threat of hunger, including increasing numbers of working people.

Injustice is not limited to economics. Across the globe, families are destroyed by war and countless people are persecuted, imprisoned, and tortured for voicing their convictions or

What's Wrong?
Read 2 Corinthians 8:8-15. What do you think Paul meant when he wrote about "a fair balance between your abundance and their need?" How do you envision this type of fair balance on a global scale today? Is global justice a reasonable goal? Why or why not? How much (if any) of our own money, possessions or security should we be willing to give up in order to have a more balanced world?

As a group, brainstorm as many examples of global injustice or imbalance as you can, and list them on a chalkboard or large piece of paper. Then, individually, assess your own lifestyle in terms of the group's list. Is there anything about your lifestyle that contributes to any of the injustices on the list? Explain. Is this aspect of your lifestyle within your power to change? If so, how? What, if anything, are you doing to heal any of the injustices listed? Share your responses in pairs or with the whole group.

practicing their faith. Can balance be restored to such a broken world? Is the simple act of sharing resources enough to overcome the enormous injustice that exists? Perhaps we feel that global justice is so far from our grasp that we cannot even fathom what a just world would look like. Fortunately, God has provided a blueprint.

GOD'S PEACEABLE KINGDOM

God's Peaceable Kingdom
Read Isaiah 2:1-4; 11:1-9; and 65:17-25 again. Select the passage that evokes the most vivid imagery for you and spend a few moments in silence to think about what the world would look like if Isaiah's words were a reality. Then express your vision artistically in a drawing, song, or poem. Share your artistry and explain its meaning.

Read Isaiah 2:1-4; 11:1-9; and 65:17-25. These beautiful words from the prophet Isaiah paint a vivid portrait of a world where God's *shalom* reigns. Isaiah spoke these words from the earlier chapters in the eighth century before Christ, when the Hebrew people faced the threat of attack from the Assyrian empire. The last reference continued the theme, most likely by one writing in Isaiah's name to the exiled community in the late sixth century. God sent Isaiah to warn the Hebrews of the consequences of their sinful behavior and complicity with their enemies and foretold the capture of Jerusalem, which eventually came to pass in 586 B.C. However, Isaiah's prophecy also contained a more hopeful message, reflected in the passages above: that God would one day rescue God's people from oppression and restore them to a life of peace and abundance, God's *shalom*.

In practical terms, what does *shalom* mean to you? How close are we to realizing the *shalom* Isaiah described? Have you ever experienced a feeling of *shalom* in your life? If so, share your story of this experience with others in your group. What factors contributed to this experience? What could you do to re-create your experience of *shalom* and extend it to others?

"Peace" is the closest English translation to the Hebrew word *shalom*, but the concept of *shalom* is much broader than an absence of war. *Shalom* encompasses the ideals of harmony and balance, sufficiency and abundance, justice and righteousness, shared and practiced by all people. But still, *shalom* means more. A gift, it is the reconciliation of God with God's people.

THE EARTH IS THE LORD'S

Read Psalm 104 and Ezekiel 34:17-22. The lyrical poetry of the psalms provides a lovely illustration of God's care for the world. It also tells us clearly that the earth and everything in it belongs to God, not to us. Psalm 104 tells of God's love for the whole environment, including air and water, mountains and valleys, grass and trees, and all the animals. Interestingly, humans are mentioned only briefly in this description of God's beloved creation.

Ezekiel used the metaphor of sheep to warn the Israelites against using disproportionate amounts of resources that God intended for everyone. He cautioned that God's "sheep" must not trample the pasture that others would eat, or foul the water that others would drink. Ezekiel declared that humans should share God's resources fairly with other humans. But when read in conjunction with Psalm 104, we might conclude that humans should also share God's resources fairly with the rest of creation.

Issues of global justice are complex enough when we think about them in purely human terms. But Scripture tells us that we cannot ignore the natural environment in our quest for balance. Unfortunately, the earth is suffering under human excesses. According to Mathis Wackernagel and William Rees of the University of British Colombia, if everyone in the world used as many resources as the average American, more than four earths would be required to supply the demand. Our rate of use stretches finite resources beyond sustainable limits.

The Earth Is the Lord's
Read Ezekiel 34:17-22. Use a Bible commentary to learn some background about Ezekiel's intended audience. How do you interpret Ezekiel's message in the context of ancient Hebrew culture? How do you interpret it in the context of our society today? Do you think Ezekiel's message says anything about our responsibility to care for non-human elements of creation? What is the impact on humans if humans fail to preserve the natural order?

How do we balance human needs with needs of other parts of God's creation? Think of situations in the news in which human needs appear to conflict with environmental concerns. Select an issue and summarize both sides. Are you more likely to agree with the "human" or "environmental" position? Why? Or, is this a false dichotomy? Explain. Think of some "both/and" solutions to environmental concerns. How do you care for creation in your daily life?

Look up the following hymns: "God, Who Stretched the Spangled Heavens," "I Sing the Almighty Power of God," and "All Things Bright and Beautiful." Sing or recite them together. What do these hymns say about God's love for all of creation? What does this imply about our responsibility to care for creation?

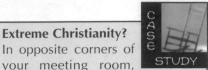

Extreme Christianity?

In opposite corners of your meeting room, place signs labeled "Iliana" and "Russ." Read Iliana and Russ's statements from the "Getting Started" section, and move to the corner corresponding to the statement that is closer to your own position. In your group, explain your choice. What are the implications of your position for living a balanced life in the world? What does it mean be a radical Christian? What are the pros and cons of doing so? Is it possible to stand up for justice without being radical? If so, how? Share your insights with the other group.

Form three small groups, each to study a different one of the following passages: Luke 9:23-25; Luke 14:25-33; and Philippians 3:7-11. In your group, read the passage and discuss what you think Jesus or Paul was trying to teach his audience. Then talk about how you interpret the passage in the context of our own society. How do you think God wants us to apply this passage? Share your results with the other groups.

EXTREME CHRISTIANITY?

Few people will argue against the existence of profound imbalances in today's world. The difficulty comes with our response to this imbalance. The four statements in the "Getting Started" section illustrate some of the frustration many of us feel when confronted with the complexity of global problems. The words of Iliana and Russ reflect the uncertainty we may experience when trying to discern God's will in responding to injustice. Just how radical does God want us to be?

Read Luke 9:23-25; 14:25-33; and Philip- pians 3:7-11. All three of these passages appear to advocate radical forms of Christian action. Jesus' words in Luke indicate that to be his followers, we must be willing to give up all we have, even our own lives. Paul's letter describes how he lost everything in order to serve Christ, but considered his losses meaningless in comparison to the salvation he gained.

Did Jesus really mean what he said? Or were his extreme words just a way to emphasize the point that we must put service to God before our desire to acquire possessions and security for ourselves? Perhaps each one of us must discern God's answer as it applies to our own life. But while we know Jesus renounced violence, he certainly seemed to affirm radical discipleship.

Martin Luther King, Jr., in his "Letter from Birmingham City Jail," responded eloquently to Christians who questioned his radical response to racial injustice with these prophetic words: "Was not Jesus an extremist for love. Was not Paul an extremist for the gospel of Jesus Christ. The question is not whether we will be extremist but what kind of extremist we will be. Will we be extremists for hate or will we be extremists for love? Will we be extremists for the preservation of injustice—or will we be extremists for the cause of justice?"

FAITHFUL RESPONSES

Read James 2:14-17 and Matthew 25:31-46. In his letter, James states his opinion quite bluntly: All talk and no action just will not cut it for Christians. Kind words alone will not fill an empty stomach. If we are truly people of faith, that faith will inspire us to tangible action whenever we encounter someone in need.

In Matthew 25:31-46, Jesus explained exactly what he expects us to do to meet the complex needs of the world. Underlying the specific actions listed (feed, clothe, welcome, visit) is the implicit directive to treat everyone we encounter as if he or she were Jesus himself. All these actions involve some sort of direct relationship between the person serving and the person in need. Perhaps Jesus is suggesting that it is not possible to practice justice in isolation. To live justly and faithfully, we must actually get to know

Prophets and Prophecy
Read Amos 2:6-16 and 6:1-7 again and reflect on them in silence. If Amos were speaking these words today, to whom would they be addressed? What meaning does Amos's prophecy have for us? Do these passages remind you of any current examples of injustice? Explain. Rewrite these passages to apply to the present and share your results with the rest of your group.

What does prophetic ministry mean to you? Think of examples of current prophets. Who are they, and what is their message? In a media-driven society where we hear so many different voices, how can we discern the difference between false prophets and true prophetic voices that speak for God?

Biblical Studies 101: *Prophets and Prophecy*

Read Amos 2:6-16 and 6:1-7. Speaking for God, Amos harshly condemned the ancient Israelites for oppressing the poor and powerless. Amos predicted utter doom for Israel if her people did not repent or step out from their complacency. We generally think of prophets as ancient seers into the future. But prophets are not just artifacts of the past, and prophecy deals with the present at least as much as the future. Walter Brueggemann, writing in *The Prophetic Imagination* (Fortress Press, 1978), asserts, "The task of prophetic ministry is to nurture, nourish, and evoke a consciousness and perception alternative to the 'dominant culture' around us." In other words, prophets challenge a society's conventional wisdom, especially if that wisdom accepts or promotes injustice. Prophetic ministry continues in the voices of people who shake us out of our complacency and inspire us to new ways of embodying God's justice.

Faithful Responses

Read Matthew 25:31-46. If Jesus told this story today, do you think he would place you with the "sheep" or the "goats?" If Jesus came to you in person and expressed an obvious need, what would you do? Why is it so difficult for us to treat poor or oppressed people the same way we would treat Jesus? If we were able to truly acknowledge the sacred worth of all people, would it change the way we respond to their needs? What prevents us from doing so?

Brainstorm specific things we can do to alleviate imbalance and injustice in the world. In a practical sense, how could you turn these ideas into action?

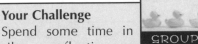

Your Challenge

Spend some time in silence reflecting on Mother Teresa's response. Pray about how God may be leading you to answer it. How is God calling you to help restore balance to God's world? How might your gifts, talents, and passions equip you to help bring justice to God's people? How do you envision your role in restoring justice and balance to creation?

Offer a group prayer, thanking God for each group member and for the spiritual growth that occurred during your time together. Pray aloud about something you learned during the study or something you feel God is challenging them to do. (Everyone should feel free to pass.) Then close by asking God for continued strength and guidance as you strive for greater balance in the midst of life's inequities and demands.

the poor and oppressed and love them just as we love Jesus.

Although no one can possibly end poverty single-handedly, as Christians together we have the responsibility and power to address the root causes of injustice on a broader scale. But how can we combat problems that are so complex? To be effective, we need to educate ourselves. We should study all we can, and talk to people who are directly involved. Get to know those who are suffering and listen to them. Work with them side by side. Join others in political advocacy for the cause of justice. And constantly seek God's guidance. Justice is more than a mission project; it is a way of life that God calls us to engage in together.

YOUR CHALLENGE

In his video series on consumerism, *Curing Affluenza* (United Methodist Communications, 1993), Tony Campolo tells the story of a woman who, inspired by Mother Teresa, wanted to give up her privileged life in the United States and go to Calcutta and share in her ministry there. According to the story, the woman wrote to Mother Teresa, expecting an enthusiastic response. After several months, she finally received this brief, but profound, reply: "Find your own Calcutta."

Where is your Calcutta? How is God calling you to serve Christ there?

CASE STUDIES

Getting Started

Use any of these cases in place of or in addition to the cases in the sessions as a means of stimulating discussion.

The Lunch Break

Kelly's phone rang for the sixth time in thirty minutes. Once again, she marked the page she was trying to read and answered the phone. This time it was her pastor, asking if she could substitute next month for a teacher recovering from surgery. A few minutes ago it was her husband, asking her to pick up their daughter from hockey practice. Before that it was her friend Julie, who was feeling a little down and just wanted someone to talk to, followed by a co-worker from her night job, asking Kelly to take an extra shift for her. Earlier it was the missions committee chair, wondering if Kelly had found housing yet for the refugee family due to arrive next week. And her first call, just as she had sat down to read, was from a collection agent about an overdue car payment. Hearing her boss knock on her door, Kelly checked her watch and saw that her lunch break was over. Exasperated, she slammed her Bible shut and prayed: "I give up, God. This is the only time I have alone all day, and it's gone. It happens every time. Everyone expects so much from me, and I just can't do it all. I'm trying to be a good Christian, but can't I have a life, too?"

- What balance issues was Kelly facing?
- Why do you think Kelly didn't simply turn off the phone during her lunch break?
- How do you think Kelly responded to each of the callers? Explain. If you were Kelly, how would you have responded? Why?
- How could Kelly find more time and space for God in her life?
- Have you, like Kelly, ever felt overwhelmed by the demands others made on you? Describe the situation. How did you find balance?

The Newcomers

Inspired by their recent study of Galatians 3:26-29, the young adult Sunday school class in a 400-member, small-town church decided to take action to respond to God's call to hospitality and inclusion. Eight months ago, a group home for developmentally-challenged adults had opened two blocks away from the church. Plans for the facility had caused considerable controversy in the neighborhood, and the church had not reached out to welcome the residents. The young adult class decided to make contact with the residents and staff, offer a weekly Bible study in their home, and invite them to attend church.

Soon, a number of residents of the group home started coming to Sunday worship, accompanied by a staff member. Before long, however, complaints started to surface from a broad cross-section of church members. Some people disliked the disruptive noises that some of the newcomers occasionally made. Others resented the fact that the group of visitors sat wherever they wanted, without respecting the fact that certain members had sat in those pews every Sunday for the last 40 years. Still others questioned why people with cognitive limitations would want to participate in worship services they probably did not understand anyway. Certain influential members of the congregation complained to the pastor that the young adult class had overstepped their bounds by inviting the residents of the group home to church. Members of the young adult class were outraged by this reaction, and complained to the pastor, accusing the congregation of hypocrisy. Eventually, the conflict escalated until people on both sides threatened to leave the church.

- What balance issues can you identify in this case study?
- How might this conflict have been prevented? Once it occurred, how might it be resolved?
- Describe the situation from the point of view of each of the following people:
    a member of the young adult class
    a long-term member of the congregation who objects to the newcomers
    the pastor
    the residents of the group home who attend the church
    the staff of the group home who accompany the residents to church
- If you were in each of their places, how would the conflict make you feel? How would you respond to the conflict?
- Have you ever experienced a similar conflict in your faith community or another group? If so, describe the situation. What caused the conflict? How was it resolved? Looking back, what could have been done differently in the situation?

Injustice: Two Responses

Rhonda had always wanted to do something to help people overcome poverty and oppression, and she joined the Peace Corps after graduating from college with a degree in agriculture. After an intense training period, she started her assignment as a livestock extension agent, working with groups of small-scale cattle herders in an isolated rural district of a large African country. Part of her work involved encouraging the herders to treat their livestock with de-worming medicine twice a year to prevent parasites. One group of herders resisted, explaining to Rhonda that they had already paid the government veterinary service for this medicine a year ago, but had never received it. The head veterinarian for the district had, in effect, stolen the money. The herders were unwilling to make such an investment again.

Rhonda was incensed that a relatively affluent official would exploit the impoverished herdsmen in this way. She had visited the head veterinarian's office just two weeks ago and knew that he had a stock of the drug available. She told the herdsmen she would visit the head veterinarian that afternoon and demand justice on their behalf. The herdsmen begged her not to, insisting that this type of corruption was part of everyday life, and that if she made trouble, they might suffer far worse consequences.

Rhonda felt torn and frustrated. On one hand, she certainly didn't want to make things worse for the people she was serving. And, her own work could be compromised if the head veterinarian turned against her. On the other hand, she was annoyed by the herders' passivity and knew they would always continue to be exploited if they did not stand up for their rights sometime. Also, treating the livestock was in the best interest of the herders and their animals.

- What balance issues can you identify in this case study?
- Describe the situation from the herders' point of view. What were their options?
- What were Rhonda's options for dealing with this situation? Describe the possible outcomes for each option. What would you have done if you were in Rhonda's place? Why?
- Have you ever experienced a situation where standing up for justice, or working for "the greater good," might cause harm to yourself or others? Explain. How did you weigh the importance of the "greater good" against the potential harm you might cause? How did you respond, and why? In hindsight, would you have responded differently? Explain.
- What, in your opinion, represents "the greater good" in this case study? Justify your answer.

Spring Break

Twelve students from the Christian Fellowship group at a small college decided to spend their spring break on a mission service trip to Haiti, helping to finish and paint a newly-built education building alongside an existing church. The students worked hard all year to raise money for all their expenses. To save money, they planned to camp out on the floor of the new building at night and eat food brought in by the women of the church. Finally, it was time to go. Although they were apprehensive and did not really know what to expect, everyone was excited.

Everything went well for the first couple of days, but by the third day, some started griping about their growing dissatisfaction. By the end of the week almost everyone's motivation had waned.

Some of the comments the students made were as follows:

"This church seems much better off than the homes down the street that are falling apart. Shouldn't we be helping the poorest of the poor?"

"The unemployment rate here is enormous. Wouldn't it have been better to just send the money and employ people here to do the work?"

"I have never seen such poverty in my life. I feel so guilty for being an American. I mean, when the week is over I can just walk away."

"I'm disappointed that we're leaving tomorrow, and I still don't know much about Haitian life. Somehow I feel like I've missed something."

"How is the paint on these walls going to make a difference in anyone's life?"

"I've eaten the same small portion of the same food for five days in a row. Don't these people realize that we're still hungry?"

"I came down here to evangelize, but the only people I've come in contact with are already Christians or are clinging to some scary folk religion and they won't listen to me."

- Why do you think the students were so dissatisfied with their experience? How important is their level of satisfaction, anyway?
- What are the issues of balance between the students' understanding of their own needs and desires and those of the residents?
- How should the students' naivete and cultural blundering be weighed against their good intentions and early enthusiasm? What would be a balanced response to that from the residents?
- Have you ever been part of a group that served on a short-term mission project? How did your experience compare? Did anything about your experience leave you feeling dissatisfied or unfulfilled? What did you learn from the experience? What was rewarding and uplifting about your trip? How did you learn to balance expectations, perceived needs, and the reality and need of the recipients?

SERVICE LEARNING OPTIONS

Enhance your group's understanding of balanced Christian living by implementing some of the service projects mentioned below.

IDEA #1: Experience Transformational Travel

Plan a cross-cultural trip to gain experience living outside of your comfort zone. Make sure you include Bible study, background about the area you will be visiting, and cultural sensitivity training as part of your preparation for the trip. (Many church organizations have mission volunteer programs that organize such trips and assist with these preparations.)

Your destination may be a developing country overseas (or in your own country), an inner-city neighborhood, or an isolated rural area. Engage in a service project in your host community that will allow you to work side by side with community members. If possible, arrange to live with a host family during your stay. Participate in their daily activities and talk with them about their customs, aspirations, and difficulties. Learn about the balance issues they struggle with every day. Establish an ongoing relationship (such as a "sister church" arrangement) between your host community and your own community of faith. After you return, give a presentation about your experience to a local church or school group. Spend time reflecting on what you learned about balance and justice. How will the experience change the way you look at the world? How will it change the way you live your life?

IDEA #2: Be an Advocate for the World's Hungry People

Bread for the World is a non-partisan, US-based, Christian citizens movement that seeks justice for the world's hungry people by organizing Christians to lobby their elected officials. Look up the organization's website *(www.bread.org)* to learn background information on world and domestic hunger issues and legislation currently before Congress that affects poor and hungry people. Invite a Bread for the World representative from your region to come and speak to your group about their work. Then choose a current issue that you feel strongly about and write letters to your elected officials, urging them to support the legislative position that helps alleviate hunger and poverty. Write a letter to the editor of your local newspaper to teach others about the issue. Visit your local congressperson's office and talk to their staff. (Bread for the World provides resources that will help you carry out these advocacy activities.) You may wish to become involved in a local Bread for the World group, or start one in your church or school.

IDEA #3: Help Prisoners Prepare for Life After Prison

Get to know the chaplain of a nearby prison or transition house for former prison inmates, and explore ways to get involved in ministry with current or recent prisoners. Consider helping with literacy programs, tutoring for high-school equivalency education, computer training, or résumé preparation. Other possibilities include helping with Bible studies or cultural programs. Work with the chaplain to undergo the necessary orientation and training and receive permission to enter the facility. Together with the chaplain, visit the institution and spend time getting to know the residents. Learn from them about justice issues they face inside and outside the prison, and how they plan to deal with societal injustices once they are released. After each visit, spend time with the chaplain to "debrief" the experience. What did you learn about balance and justice? How would you respond to some of the situations the residents face? How will your experiences influence your attitudes about prisoners and our justice system?

IDEA #4: Visit a Christian Intentional Community

A Christian "intentional community" is a group of committed Christians who have chosen to live together, or in very close-knit communities, as a way to practice their faith. Examples include monasteries or convents, a rural faith community such as the Hutterites, and urban faith communities such as Reba Place in Chicago or Church of the Savior in Washington, DC. Contact a representative of the community and arrange a visit or weekend retreat to learn about their life together. Ask a pastor to help you choose the community carefully and accompany you on the visit. While you are there, talk to the members about how they balance their responsibilities within the community and in the outside world. Learn about how they balance their relationships with God, each other, and those outside the community. Ask how they resolve conflicts with their group. If possible, work together with members on a service project. After your visit, reflect on your experience. What did you learn about balance? Would applying any of the group's practices help you lead a more balanced life?